THE WITCH'S GARDEN

Harold A. Hansen

THE WITCH'S GARDEN

Translated from Danish
by Muriel Crofts

SAMUEL WEISER, INC.
York Beach, Maine

Originally published in Danish
under the title *Heksens Urtegard*
Copyright © 1976 by Harold A. Hansen.

First English edition by
Unity Press/Michael Kesend Publishing, Ltd.
1025 Fifth Avenue
New York, N.Y. 10028.

This edition published in 1983 by
Samuel Weiser, Inc.
P.O. Box 612
York Beach, Maine 03910

Typeset in Plantin
Design by Richard Bigus

ISBN 0-87728-551-9
Library of Congress Catalog Card Number 83-60122

Printed in the U.S.A.

DEDICATED

to the memory of my brother Tage Lindy Hansen of Lexington, Massachusetts.

TABLE OF CONTENTS

FOREWORD TO THE
ENGLISH EDITION

Hansen's
THE WITCH'S GARDEN

is a remarkable book. With its clear analyses of the implications of ritualistic and superstitious drug use in European history and its excellent bibliography, it should be welcomed by a wide spectrum of scholars. It likewise will fascinate the general reader interested in the religious, social, and cultural development of Western civilization.

The recent upsurge in the study of hallucinogenic plants has helped focus scientific attention on witchcraft, sorcery, prophecy, divination, and other magical practices. Investigations of hallucinogenic and other psychoactive plants have transcended the limited fields of history and the social sciences. The potential of some of the active principles in these plants as tools in experimental psychology or even in psychiatry, and the extraordinary new vistas which their investigation has opened up in phytochemistry, have fascinated contemporary research specialists.

Quite in contrast to drugs of primitive societies inhabiting remote tropical regions, the toxic and narcotic plants so highly valued in medieval European witchcraft are widely known, and their role in superstitious practices is relatively well understood. Some of them have even become major elements in our modern pharmacopoeias. Nevertheless, it is difficult to find gathered into one volume, as reliable information on the extent of drug use in the witchcraft of Europe as can be found in *The Witch's Garden*.

This book renders a commendable service by adding to our modern library of works on hallucinogens and poisons, a readable, balanced, well-documented study on a special phase of their history and significance. This volume, which first appeared in Danish and consequently was available to a rather limited audience, can now be appreciated by a wider public through the careful translation into English by Muriel Crofts.

In order to fully understand the deep-seated influence of hallucinogens in many aspects of human affairs, a clear picture of their fundamental importance in early European civilizations must be offered. It was in this geographical area that the use of psychoactive agents and poisons went far beyond magico-religious ceremonies and curing rituals, and embraced the total philosophy of birth, of living, and of dying. The ideas underlying the practice of witchcraft—manipulation of the supernatural for good or for evil, treatment of illnesses or the induction of them, practices surrounding childbirth and protection of the newborn from malevolent elements, preparation for death and often the safeguarding of the soul after death—were characteristic of European culture during the Dark Ages and into Medieval Times. Inebriating plants made up an integral part of the witches' practices in this long period, and their influence lasted, although somewhat diluted, until relatively recent times. Even though seemingly no longer connected with use of hallucinogens, the contemporary problems experienced with the practice of exorcisms in Europe stem directly from the hallucinogenically supported witchcraft of earlier times which invaded even the religions that held Europeans so long in thralldom.

The enigma of St. Anthony's Fire is a good example of the hold which hallucinatory witchcraft maintained for hundreds of years in Europe. Ergotism, a phenomenon which mystified the ignorant and the educated alike until its natural cause—intoxication due to a parasitic ascomycete growing on rye and other grasses—was discovered. In fact, there have recently been advanced intriguing theories that the witchcraft craze in colonial New England, especially in Salem, Massachusetts, as well as the Eleusinian Mysteries of classical Greece, were manifestations of ergot poisoning.

Much of a fundamental nature can be learned from critical studies of the social, religious, political, and historical influence of the witches' brews, secret formulas, and diabolic potions so cleverly employed in so many diverse ways in medieval Europe. Hansen's contribution makes the task of evaluating this influence easier, more enjoyable, and more relevant to the sundry aspects of culture upon which the problems of witchcraft impinge.

Richard Evans Schultes, Ph.D.
Holding the chair of
Paul C. Mangelsdorf
Professor of Natural Sciences;
Director, Botanical Museum of Harvard University,
Cambridge, Massachusetts.

TRANSLATOR'S NOTE

Most of the plants mentioned in this book have long since been introduced to the North American continent and may be encountered as parts of the flora in those areas which have climatic conditions similar to those of their Old World homelands. The interested reader should consult the various check-lists of poisonous and narcotic plants available from county or state departments of agriculture, botany departments of local colleges or universities, or in publications at local public libraries.

INTRODUCTION

WHEN THE SUN

sinks into the sea and darkness broods over the land, a change takes place in the balance of power between good and evil. The Christian God, His angels and humankind hold sway in the daytime, but when the curfew bell has rung down the sun all kinds of creatures from the world of evil swarm forth: the unhallowed dead arise from their graves; demons, gnomes and elves come out from their hiding places. Worst of all, among the humans themselves there are traitors to be found: witches and warlocks who are in league with the Devil and his regiment, and with them rule over the world throughout the night, until the first rays of the sun come to the aid of the powers of good, so that men may go about their business in reasonable safety.

It was thus that people in the past understood the duality of nature and human existence, and a little of the old belief still lingers on. We feel something vaguely disquieting during eclipses of the sun, and we look with a certain distrust on anyone who works far into the night. Even if unconsciously, we insist that the boundary between the worlds of light and darkness should be respected, for we are dimly aware that incalculable misfortune would result from any change in the balance of power.

Our forefathers were convinced that this delicate balance between good and evil could only be maintained if all, without exception, remained steadfast in their faith. For war, plague and famine—God's warnings—so frequently ravaged the land that the witches bore much of the blame, for they had a foot in each camp, that of the light and that of the darkness. It is understandable that every means was tried to suppress them. But the task was difficult, for they did not choose to make themselves known and were particularly well organized, the better to protect themselves and to enable them to practise their evil deeds with greater industry.

Just as the Christian community had always been hierarchically graduated, with the Pope and the Emperor at the top and mendicant friars and serfs at the bottom, and just as the rulers of Hell had subjects varying in rank from the highest ranking archdemon down to the most wretched, almost pitiful imp, so, in the course of time, order and structure had been created in the witches' community, with a European Pope of the Witches whom all the witches had to obey. His immediate vassals, the Grand Masters of the Witches, had authority over their countries' covens, each of which was led by a local wizard.

We can follow from antiquity the gradually hardening formulation of this fantastic figment of the imag-

ination, in particular from *The Golden Ass,* in which
Apuleius (ca. 123 A.D. –?) gives a clear picture of
witches and their odious practices, to its final elabora-
tion in *Malleus maleficarum,* "The Hammer of the
Witches", 1486, written by the Dominican Friars
Heinrich Kramer and Jacob Sprenger, which in the
following centuries was diligently consulted by all who
had anything to do with witch-hunting.

At the beginning of the last century, when scientific principles were first applied to research into the history of witchcraft, the German Jacob Grimm advanced the theory that the roots of witchcraft were to be found in Germanic pagan mythology. Soldan, another German scholar, thought that it had its origins in the ancient Graeco-Roman culture. But neither these nor any other of the theories advanced at this early stage provided the witches with any *raison d'être*.

The Egyptologist Dr. Margaret Murray was the first person who managed to add flesh to the ideological skeleton of witchcraft. In her opinion the witches were worshippers of Cernunnos, the Horned God, an ancient pagan fertility god.[1] Dr. Murray maintained that the witches had kept the belief in Cernunnos alive, first during the many centuries of still heathen, but more advanced mythological concepts, and then far into the Christian era. This was not really such an impossible idea, for there are known parallels: a number of the nature deities of the Stone Age still survive to this day in Southern European superstition. And what is the duality discussed above but a continuation of prehistoric animism into the Christian era? Dr. Murray's theories were therefore very favorably received to begin with. They provided apparently rational explanations of a number of hitherto unanswered questions concerning the history and nature of witchcraft. They explained why at certain times of the year the witches had to meet on one or another of the many European sabbat mountains: the Brocken, Hecla in Iceland, Blåkulla, Lyderhorn, Tromskirke and others. Each

[1] Set forth in two main works, Murray (1921) and (1933).

nation's witches had their own meeting-place.

It also became clear that the witches' covens, whose existence the old witch-hunters had postulated, really had existed, for it was in these small congregations— of thirteen members, according to Dr. Murray—that the witches continued to practise the ancient cult. The marked uniformity in witchcraft from country to country now became understandable, for in ancient times the worship of Cernunnos extended throughout the whole of Europe.

Unfortunately, these fascinating theories have been given a rough passage by later scholars. Nor has the research of the religious historian Emanuel Linderholm,[2] who held similar views, remained undisputed. But even if criticism has proved a valuable corrective to Dr. Murray's somewhat lively imagination, it has not been able to shake either her or Linderholm's basic theories, which are, on the whole, complementary.

It is doubtful whether it will ever be possible to gain a completely clear picture of the origin of witchcraft or to reach any sort of agreement over the extent of its organization. With regard to the latter, it certainly seems doubtful whether it can be proved to have been organized on a European or even a national basis. On the other hand, it is unjustifiable to doubt, as have some of Dr. Murray's most zealous opponents, whether the witches' covens ever existed; their reality has been proved beyond a shadow of doubt by the results of a great deal of careful research. The only thing that can be said without fear of contradiction about the history of the witches is that they carried on pagan and crypto-

[2] Linderholm (1918).

Christian traditions,[3] that they were the heirs to ancient knowledge of nature's secret powers, and that they were accused—certainly often with justice—of misusing these powers to the injury of their fellow men.

The witches' knowledge of nature is far better charted than is their allegiance to this or that world of religious ideas. Both witches and monks carried on the ancient practice of herbal medicine but, let it be noted, each his own branch of it. In the monastery gardens the medicinal plants which were mainly cultivated were those which had been used as long ago as in the time of Hippocrates and Galen. The witch's herb garden, on the other hand, contained perhaps a few of these plants, but otherwise contained only herbs about which the doctors of old had been almost unanimous in their warnings, and which in the olden times were used only by wizards or poisoners. It is no coincidence that the old Latin feminine word for poisoner, *venefica*, came in time to mean specifically 'witch' in romance languages.[4]

---

[3] How old these traditions are on European soil has only become clear during the last few decades. According to Gimbutas (1974) they go back to about 7000 B.C., when, in an area bounded to the north by the Danube, to the south by Crete, to the west by Central Italy and to the east by Asia Minor, a culture arose in whose conceptual world the female and the male principles were equal. The Great Goddess and her male equivalent, the Stone Age Dionysus, are associated with the quarters of the moon and the bull's horns, with the yoni and the phallus, and together control man's birth, fate and death. This culture perished when the Indo-Europeans conquered prehistoric Europe, and the Great Goddess survived only in such forms as Hecate, Circe and Medea.

[4] Cf. many modern translations of the Bible use 'wizards' or an equivalent term where the Latin *Vulgate* has 'venefici'.

Our forefathers certainly feared witches because of their alleged pact with the Devil and their consequent malice, but they feared them just as much because they made and sold poisons and narcotic preparations to anyone who wished to buy them and had the means to pay. It might be a son who wanted his paternal inheritance earlier than it would have come to him in the course of nature, a woman in an inconveniently 'interesting' condition, or a seducer with the idea of 'charming' his unwilling victim. These aspects of the witch's activities—her bread and butter, so to speak—are interesting not merely in themselves but in particular because they provide striking examples of the similarity between the witches' community and other secret sects and orders. The Order of Templars engaged in extensive trading and finance—their enemies accused them of practising usury. The freemasons were, during the first centuries of their existence, builders and architects. The Rosicrucians, it is said, were professional alchemists and astrologers. Even today we see groups of anarchists staging hold-ups to make ends meet, Arab terrorists earning millions from successful hijackings, and the witch-like members of the Manson family living off sugar daddies while awaiting the second coming of their satanic prophet. Everywhere and at all times groups outside the established community have specialized, each in its own economic field of action, in marginal or criminal acts or a combination of both. The witches' incontestable activity as poisoners and quack doctors may be taken as indirect evidence that a form of witch organization must have existed and not merely as a fiction created by the overheated imagination of mediæval man.

It would have been interesting to have been able to examine all the various aspects of the witches' herbal knowledge and skill in this book. Unfortunately, considerations of space have obliged me to limit the subject matter to what is shown in the table of contents. Even within these limits I would scarcely have undertaken the task had others not come to my help. It is my pleasant duty to thank them here.

For information and documentation my particular thanks are due to the personnel of the New York Botanical Garden Library, the Copenhagen University Library, and the Danish Botanical Central Library and Royal Library; to Professor Dr. Helmut Möller of Göttingen, and to Hal Goldman and Peter Meloney of Lindos, Greece. For their great encouragement and help during the preparation of the manuscript my thanks go to Nanna and Volmer Christensen, Sven Langkjær, Elisabet Nordbrandt, Henrik Nordbrandt, Preben Major Sørensen and—last but not least—to my wife Jeanne and daughter Gladys Ingrid.

H. A. Hansen

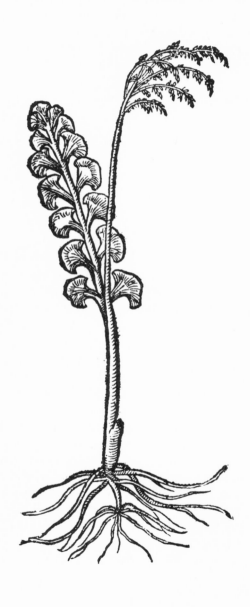

"O, mickle is the powerful grace that lies
In plants, herbs, stones, and their true qualities;
For nought so vile that on the earth doth live
But to the earth some special good doth give;
Nor aught so good but, strain's from that fair use,
Revolts from true birth, stumbling on abuse . . ."

Shakespeare, *Romeo and Juliet*, II, 3.

THE WITCH'S GARDEN

Who amongst us does not remember the mixture of
wonder, suspense and horror which we felt when as
children we heard for the first time a fairy tale about a
witch and her remote and sinister cottage in a gloomy
overgrown garden where poisonous and magic herbs
fought for room amidst ancient, twisted trees? But the
witch of the fairy tale and her surroundings never
really existed except in the realm of fantasy. Witch
and peasant lived side by side in the village. She dared
not, like the old monks and herbal doctors, plant a
garden where she could systematically cultivate her
herbs. Instead, she secretly gathered the plants she
wanted to use, either where they grew wild, or where
she cultivated them unseen in out-of-the-way places.[1]
This parcelling out of the witch's garden was similar
to that of the old farm, which often consisted of widely
separated fields, meadows and peat cuttings. One can
thus speak with an easy conscience of the witch's gar-

den, regardless of the fact that it was spread over a dozen or more places in the neighborhood.

In the following chapters a small number of plants are discussed. It has been established with certainty that in large areas of the old world such plants were employed by witches and poisoners for thousands of years, and were used, in particular, in the flying ointments with which the witches rubbed themselves before the sabbat journeys. In addition, a number of plants are discussed which certainly grew in the witch's domain, but in such remote places that she only went in search of them occasionally.

[1] The witch gathered her herbs under cover of darkness not only because she did not wish to be seen, but also because she, like her contemporaries, believed that for every medicinal and magic plant there was an optimum time to gather it, when its strength was greatest, and when loss of strength through uprooting or cutting was least. All, or nearly all, of the witch's herbs had to be gathered at night, some when the moon was waning or in eclipse, others when it was waxing, and one, the legendary Moonwort, *Botrychium lunaria*, at full moon. Since the influence of the moon on a number of biological phenomena has recently been proved, there is reason to believe that the witch knew what she was doing. "We humans are food for the moon," said a Chinese sage, and perhaps plants are as well.

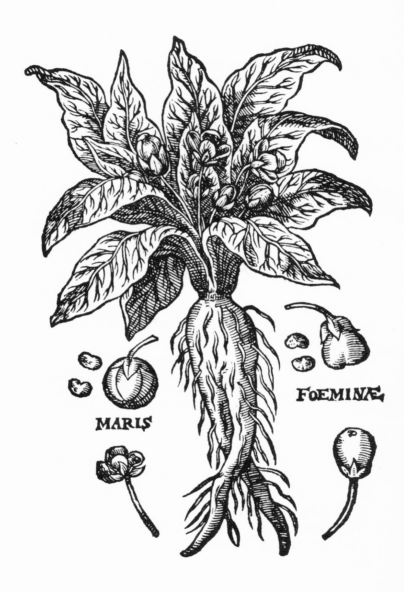

MARIS

FOEMINÆ

*"Mandrakes upon known account
have lived near an hundred
yeares . . ."*

Sir Thomas Browne's "The
Garden of Cyrus" in the *Religio
Medici.*

MANDRAKE

Mandragora officinarum. So much has been written—
and is still being written—about this plant that not
even the most industrious can hope to read it all. Nor
is it necessary to do so, for the body of tradition which
has grown up around the mandrake has not acquired
any essentially new features since the 1700s. Any modern treatment of the material can therefore only be, let
us hope, a discriminating review. This does not seem
to worry anyone: more is being written about it today
than ever before.

Mandrake is of interest in the same way as are the
Great Sea-serpent, Atlantis, El Dorado and the Proph-
ecies of Nostradamus—old hobby-horses, on which
both author and reader can ride in their sleep, but
which nobody seems willing to do without.

These and a few other topics—the evergreen growths
of popular history—all have this in common: they are
syntheses of very ancient myths. They all deal with

aspects of a former reality which may perhaps return again: man's battle against dangerous wild beasts, flight from natural castastrophes, etc. Or they stress the really fundamental aspects of human faith and hope: the finding of happiness and good fortune, the foretelling of the future. What we hoard up in our mythological storehouses is by no means accidental. The reason we find such a comparatively harmless medicinal plant as the mandrake there is because it became surrounded in time by so much mystery in folklore that it was eventually regarded as not only the most powerful but also the most dangerous of all the magical herbs. It came to represent everything that is mysterious and enticing in the strange world of plants.

The *Mandragora* species, which contain the alkaloids scopolamine and hyoscyamine, was originally indigenous to the countries in and around the Eastern Mediterranean. It is still very commonly found there, in uncultivated fields and on stony wasteland.[1] Even the Ancient Persians and Egyptians knew of the healing powers of the yellow or golden-red berries and, in particular, of the root, and certainly used both parts of the plants as aphrodisiacs. Pieces of mandrake root, no doubt love talismans, have been found together with other burial artifacts in the royal burial chambers in the pyramids, and the mandrake is discussed (to-

[1] For the guidance of enthusiasts it might be mentioned that a species of mandrake, *Mandragora autumnalis*, flowers in winter on the island of Rhodes with beautiful mauve and mauve-white blossoms. The fruit, the golden-red love-apples, ripen in May, and they should be picked and eaten straight away, for the smell, which is mentioned in the Song of Solomon, soon changes to a disagreeable stench.

gether with about 700 other medicinal plants) in the famous Ebers Papyrus from the period 1700–1600 B.C.[2]

In the Bible the fruits of the mandrake are mentioned twice.[3] In Genesis XXX, 14–16, Rachel bartered for them with Leah so that she might become fruitful with their aid, and in the Song of Solomon VII, 11–13, the lovely young Shulammite—more poetically described than any other woman on earth—invites her beloved to go with her out into the country. There she will give him her love where the mandrakes give forth their perfume, and the intent is clear that they shall make him ardent in the act of love.

The Greek doctor of classical times Theophrastus (ca. 370–328 B.C.) makes it clear that the mandrake is no ordinary plant. Before discussing the fact that the root is used, among other things, both as a soporific and an aphrodisiac, he sets forth, without, as he says,

---

[2] Frits Heide (1921). The Mandrake (Mandragora) in Ancient Egypt. *Tidsskrift for Historisk Botanik*, Vol. 1, p. 21 ff., however, disputes this identification.

[3] Botanists today are unanimous in their opinion that love-apples were the fruit of the species *M. vernalis,* but in former times when differences about the least jot or tittle in the Bible could inflame passions, scholars carried on a long and bitter feud over what was meant by the Hebrew word *dudäim:* the Easter lily, violet, blackberry and even the banana were suggested.

It may be mentioned, as a curiosity, that an English writer, Hugh J. Schonfield, in his book *The Passover Plot* claims that there is a third, though indeed hidden, reference to the mandrake in the Evangelists' story that on the cross Jesus was given a sponge soaked in vinegar to drink. Schonfield believes that this vinegar contained mandrake juice which was to have produced in the Savior a condition resembling death, so that He might the sooner be taken down

himself believing them, the measures which rhizotomists, (root-cutters), consider must be taken when gathering the plants.[4] First, three circles must be drawn with the knife in the earth around the plant. With one's face turned towards the west, the topmost part of the root can then be cut off. Next, more of the root is uncovered, but before the last bit is cut free one must dance around it, reciting as much as one can remember of the mysteries of love. A Danish scholar commented on this passage with the remark that undoubtedly the idea here was to repeat as many indecencies as possible.[5] This sounds probable, for it is a well-known fact that demons take fright and disappear if only one behaves lewdly enough.

Even Pythagoras, who was born about 582 B.C., is said to have called the mandrake an anthropomorph, that is, an herb resembling a human being,[6] and with a little effort one can also imagine that the tap-root, which is often divided, could be a little human creature or a doll. When the plant is described in the oldest Greek medical books it is most often only its medical uses that interest the authors. Not until the time of the Roman Empire were details added of its dangers and magical powers. Thus Josephus Flavius, the Jewish general, diplomat and historian, who ended his days in Rome about the year 95 A.D., relates that in a valley near the Dead Sea there grows a wonderful plant which

from the cross and then, with the aid of doctors, be brought back to life. The plan miscarried when one of the soldiers—unexpectedly and irregularly—stuck the lance into His side.

[4] Theophrastus, II, pp. 259–261.
[5] Heiberg (1917), p. 11.
[6] Dioscorides, IV, 76, pp. 189–191.

at night emits a glowing red light.[7] It is difficult to get close, for the plant withdraws when it notices someone approaching. But if one succeeds in pouring urine or menstrual blood over it, it will keep still. Direct contact with the plant is deadly dangerous, but all the same it is possible to get it out of the ground. First, one should dig carefully around it until only the nethermost tip of the root is still stuck fast in the earth. Then one tethers a dog to the root and moves away. When the dog tries to follow its master it drags the plant from the ground, but immediately dies as a vicarious sacrifice for its master, who can now safely possess himself of the costly plant. The method is complicated, but still worth the trouble and the price of a dog, for the plant has the property of being able to drive out demons, who fly in terror if it is merely brought into the vicinity of people who are possessed.

Josephus' statement that the plant shines in the dark is not entirely without foundation. In certain weather conditions it may happen that small chemical particles in the night dew and on the surface of the berries combine together to produce a faint glow of light. A similar phenomenon may be observed on warm, northern summer nights where blueberries are growing.

A few generations later Aelian introduces new details into the picture.[8] The mandrake cannot be seen by day because it hides itself among other plants. At night, however, it shines like a star in the darkness and one can mark the spot where it is growing and the next day be certain which plant is the mandrake, even if it looks

---

[7] Josephus Flavius, VII, 6, 3.
[8] Aelian, XIV, 27, vol. 3, pp. 189–191.

exactly like its innocent neighbor. Then one ties up a starving dog to the root and, before moving away, sets a fragrant portion of fried meat just out of its reach. The starving animal quickly tries to get to the meat, but dies just as it draws the mandrake from the earth. The corpse should be buried where the plant was growing, and a burial ceremony should be carried out in honor of the animal which laid down its life so its master could acquire the mandrake.

Elsewhere it is stated that the dog does not necessarily have to die. Only if it enters the first of the previously mentioned circles is its fate sealed. But this respite for dogs in the folklore of the mandrake did not last long, for soon it was said that the mandrake *always* uttered such a blood-curdling shriek when it was pulled up that whoever heard it would die of terror. From then on only *black* dogs were used to pull it from the ground. But they were ill-fated from the start, for the Creator would scarcely have given them such an ill-omened color if they had not been evil beasts that richly deserved to die.

Because its shape resembled that of a human being, the mandrake gradually became regarded as a sinister living creature. The stages of this transformation are not known in detail. The legend of Jason's 'dragon men' may have contributed toward this view, but probably the most important source is a story from early Christian times. This tale relates that the mandrake was originally a preliminary study for Man which God rejected after He had created Adam from the red earth of Paradise.[9] The reason the plant is so rare is

[9] This tradition later supplied poetry with new images and meta-

+ CREATION MYTH

that it still prefers to grow near the Garden of Eden, which lies far away on top of a mighty mountain somewhere in the unknown lands of Asia.[10]

This interesting account did not, however, prevent cultivation of the real mandrake plant in gardens north of the Alps. Here, particularly on German lands, new traditions became associated with it and some of the old ones came to be regarded as superstitions and were forgotten, although they were perhaps written down before this happened and are therefore still known. A radical innovation in the popular belief was that the mandrake, now also known under the names 'gallows-man' and 'dragon-doll',[11] can only grow at the foot of the gallows and only comes up where either urine or semen from a hanged man has wetted the earth. But, it is pointed out, not just any gallow-bird's drippings have the power to produce the mandrake. The hanged man must have been what in Danish is called 'a pure

---

phors—cf. John Donne's "The Progresse of the Soule", from the beginning of the 17th century.

[10] The mediæval bestiaries relate that elephants, when mating time approaches, move eastwards in the direction of the Garden of Eden, the reason being that the male is so virtuous by nature that the female can only tempt him to mate if she can lure him to eat the fruits of the mandrake which are to be found in and around Paradise.

[11] The mandrake gradually acquired many names: in Danish, in addition to gallows-man and dragon-doll it was also called dollwort, poor sinner's flower, executioner's root and torturer's root.

The name dragon-doll may have originated from a popular misinterpretation of the second syllable of Mandragora—as the Danish verb *drage* (to draw or attract), or may be derived from the German *Drache* (also *drage* in Danish), which means both the fabulous dragon and a demonic creature which, according to popular belief, brings riches to him who can gain power over it

youth' (the nearest English equivalent being something like 'a right lad'). In this connection it means that in life he had been an arch-scoundrel, one who acquired his thieving nature in his mother's womb, so that he had never done anything else but steal.[12]

Like everything that has to do with crime, torture and death, a place of execution is surrounded by mystery and horror. It was not everyone's cup of tea to venture out to the gallows hill to dig mandrake from earth which also housed the moldering remains of rogues who had been hanged, beheaded or broken on the rack. Most of the people who wanted to acquire a mandrake would certainly have preferred to buy it instead. A new mandrake cost a great deal of money, but that is not surprising considering its origins and the qualities attributed to it. It made its owner in-

---

by means of magic spells. *Dukkeurt* ('dollwort', translated literally, in German *Dollwurz*) is found for the first time in the Danish language in Hans Tavsen's translation of Genesis. The designations 'poor sinner's flower', 'executioner's root' and 'torturer's root' are interesting as they suggest that the torturer and his victim had more to do with the mandrake than has generally been supposed. One may assume that the soporific drink which the executioner sometimes gave the condemned before torture or execution sometimes contained mandrake berry juice mixed with wine or vinegar. The reputedly frequent appearance of the plant beneath the gallows thus becomes credible and an apparently purely superstitious feature of the legend is given a natural explanation.

[12] If a woman stole while she was pregnant, the child's soul suffered damage: The boy became in time a 'pure youth' or a 'right lad', or the girl a whore. It is because of these 'poor sinners', destined for the gallows, that there are mandrakes of both sexes. According to another folk tradition the word 'pure' should be taken literally: The mandrake is produced in this case by the involuntarily released seed of a chaste youth who was hanged though innocent.

vulnerable in battle and granted him deadly accuracy in the use of weapons. It cured him of all sicknesses and was particularly effective against those he brought home from the battlefield of love. It helped him discover hidden treasure, so that he quickly became a wealthy man, greatly esteemed by his fellow men and lucky in love, for no woman could resist the compelling power of the mandrake.

A talisman that could do all this and more had to be handled with the greatest care or it became useless, even dangerous. The old hatred toward mankind for being replaced in God's grace still lived in the mandrake. (This superstition did not seem to be influenced by the fact that the mandrake of the gallows-man and that of the Garden of Eden might hardly be thought to have much to do with each other.)

The newly acquired mandrake should be bathed in wine, wrapped in red and white silk and covered with a black velvet cloak. Every weekday it should be bathed again and afterwards fed, but there is considerable disagreement about what it should have to eat. The majority inclined to the opinion that it was sufficient if it received communion bread which one had refrained from swallowing at the altar-rail. Others thought that 'a portion of fasting spittle' was what it liked best, and there were learned folk who insisted that the mandrake should, above all, be fed with the red earth of Paradise, from which it and we and, indeed, the whole multiplicity of creation originated. This last idea, however, seems hardly to agree very well with the fact that mediæval alchemists coveted the mandrake precisely because it contained some of this unique kind of earth, which was so necessary as a catalyst in the production of the Philosopher's Stone.

It sometimes happened that a dragon-doll would become tired of its master, no matter how well he had treated it. In that case it would not work, and one might as well sell it straight away, for otherwise it became malicious and caused misfortune. Moreover, anyone who owns a mandrake becomes uneasy at keeping it, for it is a dangerous thing to have appropriated to oneself more good fortune than one is entitled to. It is a sin, for it makes others suffer, since the sum of good fortune in the whole world is constant: If one takes too much, another will have too little. But to get rid of a mandrake could be difficult, especially if it was old and had already served many masters. For the same applied to it as to Cyprianus: It could not be given away and could only be sold for less than what one had paid for it. When the price had fallen to the value of the smallest coin in the realm it was impossible to find a buyer and when the owner died it had to go with him into his coffin. On the Day of Judgment it would stand before God at its owner's side and claim his share of eternal life.

When belief in the mandrake was at its strongest, in the 16th and at the beginning of the 17th centuries, doubts also began to be expressed. John Gerard (1547–1607), whose herbal was published in 1597, reels off, with obvious disapproval, various superstitions concerning the mandrake, and closes with the following admonition: "All which dreames and old wives tales you shall henceforth cast out of your books and memory; knowing this, that they are all and everie part of them false and most untrue: For I my selfe and my servants also have digged up, planted, and replanted very many, and yet never could either perceive shape of man or woman, but sometimes one streight root, sometimes two, and often six or seven branches comming from the maine great root, even as Nature list to bestow upon it, as to other plants. But the idle drones that have little or nothing to do but eat and drinke, have bestowed some of their time in carving the roots of Brionie, forming them to the shape of men and women: which falsifying practice hath confirmed the errour among the simple and unlearned people, who have taken them upon their report to be the true Mandrakes."[13]

Gerard was not the first to protest. He himself refers to Dr. William Turner, who in 1551 had said something similar in the first part of his herbal, and the human form of the mandrake had been denied as early as in *The grete herball* of 1526.[14] But three English swallows do not make a Danish summer, and in Denmark the belief was strongly upheld right into the

[13] Woodward (1927), pp. 85–86.
[14] Cf. Arber (1938), p. 123.

18th century, when the ironical Holberg in *Witchcraft or False Alarm* lets Apelone declare that "when a wizard begets a son, it will be a dragon-doll which will later attract money to its mother." Not until the introduction of compulsory education did belief in the mandrake legend begin to die out. And yet it still lingers in places. Only a few years ago Danish television broadcast an interview with an old man from South Jutland who claimed, in deadly earnest, that one of his neighbors practised evil witchcraft and went as far as to set his mandrake on people he didn't like!

It is uncertain whether the mandrake was ever cultivated by Danish witches, but in Central and Southern Europe both the fruit and the roots were used as ingredients in aphrodisiacs and flying ointments. It is doubtful, however, whether the witches in the South always understood that the dragon-doll of the gallows hill and the beautiful little herb were identical.[15]

In Denmark the plant thrives only when carefully cultivated. The seeds are sown in light sandy soil shortly after the berries ripen. The herbs are transplanted carefully, about August, to a sheltered, sunny and well-drained plot, which is covered lightly with sprigs of spruce in the autumn.

---

[15] Neither the mandrake nor the dragon-doll is discussed in any mediæval Danish text, but belief in mandrake superstitions may have reached Denmark far earlier than written sources would suggest. A far less important magic ingredient, *Staphylea pinnata*, 'bladder-nut' (Danish blærenød), found its way to the North as early as in the Roman Iron Age; cf. M. B. Mackeprang's "Om et Træskrin med Amuletter og undergørende Planter" ("A Wooden Chest with Amulets and Miraculous Plants") in Fra National-musæets Arbejdsmark, 1936.

As far as the dragon-doll is concerned, it survives only in the comic-strip character Mandrake, created by Lee Falk, an American journalist. Falk's Mandrake is a mighty magician who, since 1934 when the series began, has been engaged to Narda, a beautiful but naive blonde. The relationship has been unfruitful so far.

*"Among other herbs which are
poisonous and harmful, Henbane
is not the least, so that the common
man, not without fear, should
spit at that herb when he hears its
name spoken, not to mention when
he sees it growing in great quantity
where his children are running
at play."*

Simon Paulli, *Flora Danica*, 1648.

Henbane

Hyoscyamus niger. When the Spaniards brought the potato and tomato to Europe in the 16th Century, it took several generations before people could bring themselves to accept them as the good and nourishing foods that they are. This was due to the fact that these two American members of the nightshade family resembled far too closely their notorious European relations, mandrake, deadly nightshade, thornapple and, last but not least, henbane. They *must* be poisonous, people thought. And so they are, but the poison, the alkaloid solanine, is found in the parts of the plants which we do not eat.

If you let a potato plant and a henbane plant grow up side by side, you can see straight away how much they resemble one another, but also what differences there are. Such a comparison will certainly not be to the advantage of the henbane with its grey-green, closely growing leaves, sticky and hairy, and its peculiar yellow, almost corpse-colored, violet-veined flowers which remind one most of all of the 'evil eye'. With such characteristics in addition to its unpleasant smell, the plant is a kind of Mr. Hyde to the potato's Dr. Jekyll. Apparently the henbane has no hidden virtues like the potato with its edible subterranean root tuber, but nevertheless it is a useful though dangerous plant, for all its parts contain the alkaloid hyoscyamine, and the seeds contain scopolamine as well. Both these dangerous poisons can be used in the service of good as well as of evil.

Even the Ancient Egyptians knew of henbane, and, like several other of the witches' herbs with which we are dealing, it is discussed in the Ebers Papyrus. It is described as a useful but dangerous plant by nearly all the ancient herbalists, and a little of the mystery which surrounded the mandrake rubbed off on henbane. Aelian, who is, incidentally, not always a reliable source, states that in digging up henbane almost the same measures were taken as for mandrake, except that it was not a dog but a bird that was tethered to the plant.[1]

The Linnean generic name is a slight variation of the Ancient Greek name *hyoskyamos*, which means pig bean. According to Otho Brunfels (1488–1534), the famous German doctor and herbalist,[2] the name refers to the fact that pigs get cramps when they eat

---

[1] Aelian, II, p. 251.

[2] Brunfels (1532), Chap. 135. The earliest known Danish name, *bylnæ* (Modern Danish *bulmeurt*), was used in mediæval manuscripts side by side with the mediæval Latin *Iusquiamus*. Danish popular names are not always flattering: toothwort, soothingwort, blessing-wort, sleeping-grass, but also the devil's pouch or nuts, dog-piss root and cat-lye. The German name, *Bilsenkraut*,

henbane. In Greece, on the other hand, the opinion is still held that the generic name derives from Homer's tale of the sorceress Circe turning the crew of Odysseus into swine with a drink of henbane.[3] As it is impossible to tell which explanation is correct, one may choose with an easy conscience to believe the latter, partly because it is the more diverting and partly because it may well have a grain of truth in it.

In the works of Apollonius Rhodius (3rd century B.C.) and Ovid (43 B.C.–17 A.D.) as well as of Homer, there are stories of magic drinks with effects which indicate that the alkaloid hyoscyamine was the most active ingredient. The first two authors mentioned above give detailed descriptions of the way in which Circe and her brother's daughter Medea, who was equally skilled in the magic arts, gathered their magical herbs.[4] There can scarcely be any doubt that these two sinister mythical figures were based on actual people—contemporary Greek witches who knew the hidden dangerous powers of henbane.

It should be mentioned here that there are in fact twelve to fourteen distinct species of henbane, of which

gave its name to the Bohemian city of Pilsen where, in the Middle Ages, there were large fields of henbane whose crushed seeds were added to the beer to make it more intoxicating—the 'Pilsener' of those days must have been really powerful!

[3] Of Circe's magic drink, Homer (Odyssey, 10th Book) says only that it contains 'the juice of magical herbs'. The identification with henbane rests exclusively on the fact that this herb contains alkaloids which can produce in its victims the illusion of having been turned into an animal.

[4] Cf., for example, Apollonius Rhodius, *Argonautica*, III, 840–68 and Ovid's *Metamorphoses*, in several places in Book 7.

only three, however, were important medical and magical herbs. Two of them, *Hyoscyamus albus*, white henbane, and *H. aureus*, golden henbane, are found only in the countries around the Mediterranean, and it was these two in particular that were used by Circe's and Medea's mortal prototypes. The third, *H. niger*, the common henbane, is indigenous further north in regions with a continental climate around the Caspian Sea. It is this species which in time spread to Western and Northern Europe and reached Denmark at a quite early date, so that Danish mediæval doctors—and witches—were able to use it—each in their own way.

Today henbane is very commonly found, particularly in uncultivated places and often as a relic of former cultivation in the ruins of castles and monasteries. It sometimes happens that it appears suddenly in places where it has never been known to grow before. It is then discovered that in the preceding year a layer of earth was disturbed over old building sites through digging or plowing.

The medical historian Jens Lind (1874–1939), compared these still fertile henbane seeds from long vanished ages with stone or bronze artifacts. "I am not saying, however," he wrote, "that the same seeds have lain at Sjørring, for example, since the year 1086 when the royal castle was demolished; one must assume that a few plants sprang up from time to time, when they had the chance, and thus renewed the earth's stock of seeds . . ."[5] In fact, later research has shown that henbane seeds buried in deep, airless strata of earth can remain viable for many hundreds of years, so the possibility cannot be ruled out that the plants seen by Jens Lind (in 1915) had germinated from seeds at least 800 years old.[6] One cannot help recalling the old stories of 'mummy wheat', of toads that jump out when stones or tree-trunks are split, and of newts which, after lying in a state of hibernation for hundreds or perhaps thousands of years in the ice, are freed and awaken to life during an unusually heavy thaw.

Did the priestesses of the Delphic Oracle prophesy under the influence of smoke from burning henbane seeds? Henbane was called *Herba Apollinaris* in ancient times, and modern scholars are unanimous in agreeing that one of them, Pythia, prophesied in a state of ecstasy produced by narcotics, so the probabilities are in favor of the old tradition being reliable.

[5] Lind (1918), p. 86 ff.
[6] The research was carried out by the botanist Søren Ødum and summarized by him in an article in the periodical *Skalk*, No. 4, 1964, pp. 18–26.

The Ancient Gauls are said to have used henbane juice as poison for their spears and arrows and, after monkshood, henbane was a favorite of the poisoners of antiquity and the Middle Ages. In more recent times poisoners have gradually gone over to using more 'convenient' means such as arsenic or strychnine, but even in the present century henbane poison has been in the news in connection with a murder case: The notorious English murderer Dr. Crippen was condemned to death and hanged in 1910 for having killed his wife with hyoscine-hydrobromide.

Henrik Smid recounts that fish can be caught "if cakes or small, round pellets are made with these seeds and thrown into water where there are fish, and when the fish eat them they go wild, leap up, turn belly up and thus may be caught by hand as long as they remain in this wild state."[7] He also tells us, in the same text, that mercenaries and gypsies who want to steal chickens dope them with the fumes of smoldering henbane seeds. Simon Paulli, in a more detailed account of this practice, says "the fact that this henbane seed has such power to make one's head heavy and to make one sleep is pretty well known to the camp-followers who roam the countryside or follow closely on the heels of the troops who march ahead of them. In order to steal a farmer's chickens skilfully and easily, they add henbane seeds to a pot of burning coals which is slipped into the chicken house. Chickens roosting on the rafters fall down and appear to be dead when the smoke reaches them. In this manner they deceive the poor simple farmer."[8]

[7] Henrik Smid (1577), 16.
[8] Paulli (1648), p. 253, No. 103.

There has been a tendency to lay most of the blame for the distribution of hemlock and henbane through the Scandinavian countries on the gypsies. Their role in this respect is almost certainly exaggerated, however. In any case, they must share much of the honor with the witches, camp-followers and other wretches who traded in or used henbane seeds, each in his own way, long before the gypsies got so far north.[9]

Henbane has been used from earliest times to produce pain-killing drugs. It has, like hemlock and mandrake, been used to alleviate the sufferings of those sentenced to death, particularly during the torture which often preceded the actual execution, especially in the case of gross offenders: coiners, sodomites, regicides and, of course, witches.[10]

But henbane is not only capable of relieving bodily pain. It can bring oblivion, or at any rate the feeling that that which has happened, is happening now, or

[9] It is more probable that the gypsies were the first to deal in seeds of *Cannabis sativa*, hemp, and to teach our ancestors the narcotic properties of hemp. Henrik Harpestræng, who died in 1244, discusses the plant, but whether it was already in use in his day as a euphoric drug is very doubtful. The hemp plant is of Central Asian origin but reached India long before the gypsies migrated from that country. It has been cultivated in Central Europe since the Stone Age and can thrive in Denmark, producing a large amount of tetrahydrocannabinol, the substance that induces the intoxication. But as a rule the northern summers are too short and too cold for the plant to seed. It has frequently been necessary to import new supplies of seed, as its germination capacity disappears after three or four years in primitive storage conditions. The roving gypsies, who have most probably always used hemp as a euphoric, would have found it easy to handle this trade, and there are many indications that over long periods of time they had almost a monopoly of the supply of hemp seed to Scandinavia.

may happen in the future, is of no importance. One accepts the situation uncritically and allows oneself to be led or misled into anything. Some scholars believe henbane was the active ingredient in the extraordinary drink of oblivion which Grimhild hands to Gudrun in the Gudrun Lay, so that she not only forgets that her husband Sigurd has been murdered, but also ceases to hate Grimhild, who brought about the murder, and even willingly becomes the bride of Attila, King of the Huns:

> *"Grimhild offered me a full cup,*
> *the taste was cool and gave sweet forgetfulness*
> *it gained added strength from the well-springs of Urd,*
> *ice-cold sea-water and hog's blood.*
>
> *Poured to me in the drink were all kinds of runes,*
> *red and acrid, without will was I,*
> *Haddingland's fish of the heather,*
> *husked ear of corn, entrails of roe-deer.*
>
> *There was in the drink killing and malice,*
> *scorched acorns, all kinds of roots,*
> *the hearth's ashes, innards of offerings,*
> *swine's sweet liver, which weakens strife"* [11]

Henbane must have been among the 'all kinds of roots', it is claimed, for of the plants which could have

[10] Was it compassion or the desire to keep order in the ranks that motivated the authorities?

[11] Translated from Martin Larsen's "Den ældre Edda og *Eddica Minora*". Copenhagen, 1943, 2nd vol., p. 153.

produced Gudrun's condition it is believed to have been the only one which had already reached the North at the time of the Sagas. Now the literary historians are quite convinced that the ancient lay comes from a lost Burgundian source. If this is true the hypothesis immediately becomes less valid, for down in Burgundy other herbs could also have been involved.

The herb was included in the witches' flying ointments, and some rather doubtful sources claim that when new people were to be made into witches, henbane juice was mixed in the cup of welcome. Under the influence of this drink the victims were led to take part in the sabbat rites in such a compromising condition that there was no possibility of backing out afterwards.

The time of witches is past, but the sinister history of henbane continues: The Anti-Slavery Society, the international organization for the prevention of the white slave trade shows in one of its reports that narcotics containing hyoscyamine are an important weapon in the hands of the criminals who occupy themselves with this villainous traffic in human life.

*"The name Belladonna originates
from the fact that the said drops
give to the woman who desires to
please, the eyes of a Medusa, large,
staring and hypnotic."*

Christian Elling, *Shakespeare, an
Insight into his World and its
Poetry*, 1959.

DEADLY NIGHTSHADE

Atropa belladonna. This Southern European and Near
Eastern nightshade can thank Linnaeus for its present
botanical name. The great naturalist was so familiar
with the nature and properties of plants that he was
almost always able to find strikingly appropriate names.
Atropa belladonna is a good example of this. The generic
name refers to the Greek Fate Atropos, the inflexible
one, who cuts the thread of life—deadly nightshade
was often the scissors in her hand. The species name
recalls another story, namely that the herb has also been
a servant of beauty and love, for 'belladonna' is its old
popular Italian name and refers most probably to the
fact that the ladies of the South once used deadly nightshade juice, which contains atropine, dissolved in water
to dilate their pupils.[1] Large, dreamy eyes have always
had a fascination for the opposite sex. In the new name
Linnaeus captured the essentials of the plant and also
handed down to posterity:

".. . a moving old picture:
Death and Love
together it represented."

Before Linnaeus' time deadly nightshade was included in the genus *Solanum,* and it was known under
a number of specific names which almost amounted to
terms of abuse and which in any case clearly indicated
the reputation which the plant had gained in the course
of time: *furiale*—raving, *mortiferum*[2]—fatal, *laethale*—
lethal, *hypnoticon*—hypnotic or spellbinding and *somniferum*—soporific. The popular names were of the
same kind: sorcerer's cherry, witch's berry, murderer's berry and dwaleberry. The latter, in Danish
dvalebær, is extremely old, for 'dwaleberry' and
'dwale' are also English mediæval names for the plant,
and as the word *dvale* (trance) is of Old Norse origin, it

[1] John Gerard wrote that the name referred to the fact that Italian
ladies used a solution of the juice in water to remove redness from
the cheeks. Another source maintains that the reddish-purple juice
of the berries was used as a rouge for the cheeks of the pale Italian
ladies. A popular tradition has it that the plant is called belladonna
because it is a magical herb which sometimes changes into a di-
vinely beautiful woman whom, unfortunately, it is mortally dangerous to meet. Finally, it has been claimed that the Romans
dedicated the herb to the goddess Bellona, whose priest drank
deadly nightshade juice before the ceremonies connected with
her worship. With the advent of Christianity the goddess was
forgotten and the name of the herb was corrupted from 'Bellona's
herb' to belladonna. The possibilities do not end here. Jules
Michelet, the Frenchman who wrote with so much insight and
understanding about witches, was of the opinion that the name
arose because deadly nightshade was the herb of 'the good women',
the beautiful women', that is, of the wise women and the witches.
[2] *Solanum mortiferum.*

rtrance - berry

is conceivable that *dvalebær* was in common use in the North before the Scandinavian migration to England took place.

Deadly nightshade is a perennial herb with a sturdy branched stalk which grows up to three feet tall, with elliptical oviform leaves and brown-purple, bell-shaped flowers. Its shining black berries are the size of preserve cherries, containing a large number of seeds and a dark, inky, very sweet juice. All parts of the plant are poisonous. The main alkaloid is hyoscyamine and the plant also contains small amounts of atropine[3] and scopolamine, with traces of apoatropine and belladonnine, which have somewhat different effects. The sweet-tasting berries are a great temptation to children, and unfortunately cases of poisoning, with fatal results, are reported nearly every year, particularly from Southern Europe. Mild cases of poisoning are manifested in high spirits and the same feeling of timelessness that marks the first stage of intoxication through hashish. The subsequent deep sleep is often accompanied by erotically colored dreams. Poisoning of medium severity produces a feeling of dryness in the throat with subsequent itching and irritation, together with later nausea and giddiness followed by deep sleep.[4] Severe poisoning causes paroxysms of rage, blindness and paralysis, then coma occurs, usually

[3] Later in the text it is stated that during the war deadly nightshade was the crude drug used in the production of atropine. This is because the hyoscyamine in the fresh plant changes into the chemically similar atropine when the plant is dried. The difference between the two alkaloids is so small that, according to Wagner (1970) pp. 56–57, it is not possible to express it by chemical formula.

followed by death from paralysis of the respiratory system.

That prognosis in cases of severe poisoning is so poor is due to the fact that the poison is broken down so slowly that it is difficult for doctors to keep patients breathing until the process is completed.

Fortunately, deadly nightshade is a rare plant in Denmark. It is found only in a few places on the coasts of the Little Belt and at Moseby on Falster Island. Strangely enough, it is not mentioned in the old Danish medical books or herbals. If the monks and later herbalists knew the plant, they did not wish to own it. It was risky to use and there were less dangerous herbs which could be used for the same purposes. "If you will follow my counsel," says John Gerard, "deal not with the same in any case, and banish it from your gardens, and the use of it also, being a plant so furious and deadly; for it bringeth such as have eaten thereof into a dead sleep, wherein many have died."[5]

Deadly nightshade has not been clearly described by any of the writers of antiquity whose books have come down to us, but a mandrake species, morion, is discussed in a way which makes it probable that deadly nightshade is the herb in question.[6] We also learn that the maenads of the Dionysian orgies, with *dilated* eyes cast themselves into the arms of the god's male wor-

---

[4] At this stage loss of control of the facial muscles may occur which has led historians to assume that the so-called 'sardonic laughter'— in the original meaning of the term—is produced by deadly nightshade poisoning.

[5] Woodward (1927), p. 74.

[6] The third of the mandrakes, which Dioscorides (IV, 76) describes, is in all probability deadly nightshade.

shippers, and that at other times, eyes *flaming* with wildness, they threw themselves onto all the men they met on their way, to tear them apart and devour them. Descriptive adjectives are of little value as proof, but they *may* indicate that the wine of the Bacchanals was sometimes mixed, not only, as we shall hear later, with thornapple juice, but also with the juice of deadly nightshade.

Presumably it was because the symptoms of poisoning were so easily recognizable that deadly nightshade was not used for murder as frequently as some related herbs.

Deadly nightshade has played a role in military history on two occasions—the first time as a poison, the second time as an antidote. According to the English doctor and herbalist Nicholas Culpeper (1616–1654), there is a strange example of this plant's fateful consequences in Buchanan's *History of Scotland*, which describes the destruction of Sweno's army after it invaded Scotland. This happened because the Scots, in agreement with the armistice conditions, sent mead to the Danes which, however, was "mixed with the Juice of a poisonous Herb, Abundance of which grows in Scotland, called Sleepy Night-shade." The Danes became so drunk on the mead that the Scots were able to fall upon and kill the majority of them while they slept, so that there were scarcely enough of them to bring their king to safety. The Danish king Sweno was in reality Svein Knutson, King of Norway 1030–1035, who tried to win Scotland from Duncan the First. The Scottish leader on this occasion was Earl Macbeth, the model for the protagonist in Shakespeare's tragedy of the same name.

The second time was in 1943. It came to the ears of the Allies that German chemists had produced a nerve gas that was both odorless and colorless, a swift killer. They were therefore obliged to lay in large stocks of atropine from deadly nightshade—the only known antidote to the gas. The Germans never used this sneaky weapon, but that could not be foreseen.

Deadly nightshade was used in various witch's brews and particularly in many flying ointments from Germany and France. Whether the Scandinavian witches used the brew is uncertain.

The plant is best cultivated in half shade on chalky, well fertilized soil which is sheltered from the wind. As the germination percentage is very low it is most practical to sow the seeds in seed-beds for later transplanting to an area so well hedged-in that no accidental poisoning can occur.

"The whores administer to those who have the misfortune to fall into their hands half of five grammes of these seeds in order to profit from their madness."

Von Aphelen, *General Natural History*, 1767.

THORNAPPLE

Datura stramonium. Datura or, more correctly 'dhatura', is derived from the Sanskrit word *dhat*, which was the name of a poison made from *Datura metel*, an Indian species of thornapple. Linnaeus, who did not generally favor exotic designations, accepted this as a generic name because he imagined that it contained a Latin root, *dare*, meaning to give, perhaps in its prescriptive sense implying, for example, the giving of thornapple juice as a cure for impotence.

The genus has numerous representatives both in the Old World and the New. In the Old World the species are herbaceous, but some of the American species are small trees and bushes. They have in common the fact that they contain the alkaloids hyoscyamine, scopolamine and atropine, substances found in all parts of the plant; indeed, the flowers alone are so narcotic that their very scent can have a stupefying effect and cause mild poisoning. This fact should not, however, mislead anyone into believing the fable of poor, abandoned Lakmé, who in Delibes' opera commits suicide by inhaling "the poisonous scent of the thornapple tree"—such a death would have taken too long.

D. stramonium, the European thornapple, has gradually become rather a rare plant but is still to be found here and there growing in refuse dumps and in places where it has escaped from gardens. It is an annual, easily recognizable by its smell, its white, funnel-shaped flowers and by its fruit, 'apples' as big as large walnuts and closely covered with spines. Small children are sometimes fatally poisoned after having eaten the seeds which, when unripe, are sweetish and palatable and, unfortunately, easy to get at, as the spines of the fruit do not become stiff and prickly until the seeds are ripe.

The original home of the plant is believed to have been in the areas surrounding the Black Sea and the Caspian Sea. It is something of a mystery when and in what circumstances it reached Europe. It is not hard to imagine that a plant with spined seed capsules, which would easily become lodged in the fur of animals, could have reached the climatic boundaries of its growth area back in the hoary days of antiquity. But even though it was known and discussed by the ancient writers of herbals and medical books, it seems to have been unknown in the Middle Ages and early Renaissance, for no mention of it is to be found either in the medical writings of the monks or by the great writers of the 1500s: Fuchs, Bock, Brunfels and others. John Gerard wrote in 1597 that thornapples were still rare curiosities in England, and Henrik Smid (1577) and Simon

Paulli (1648) apparently did not know the plant. A well-known Austrian writer, A. *Ritter* v. Perger, advanced the theory in 1864 that gypsies brought *D. stramonium* to Europe, and that "all the gypsies' arts were based mainly on an exact knowledge of the juices of the thornapple."[1] These suppositions do not seem to have been more closely examined but it is apparently correct that this herb and the gypsies arrived in Europe about the same time.

Most of the writers of antiquity feared the thornapple and warned their readers against it. Theophrastus says[2] that anyone who consumes $3/20$ of an ounce (4.2 grams) of the root will feel like a devil of a fellow; twice this dose will produce hallucinations and temporary madness; three times the dose will make him permanently insane, and four times as much will cause death. Both Dioscorides[3] and Pliny repeat this, and the latter adds[4] that the juice has been used as spear poison and that the thornapple, which he calls 'manicon', the maddening herb, has other innocent-sounding names given to it by people who, from evil motives, wish to conceal its true nature.

The question of the 'true nature' of the thornapple gave rise to many conjectures and more or less fantastic stories. When a French diplomat, on returning home from Persia some time in the 17th century, reported that bees who sucked the nectar of the Persian datura produced honey so poisonous that a spoonful of it was enough to kill a person, he was certainly exaggerating.

---

[1] Perger (1864), p. 183.
[2] Theophrastus, IX, xi, 6 (2nd volume, p. 273).
[3] Dioscorides, IV, 74, p. 470.
[4] Pliny, XXI, 179 (6th volume, pp. 287–289).

But it is a proven fact, as Dioscorides wrote,[5] that 'meli pontikon', honey from Pontus, the land of the poisonous herbs, at certain times of the year made those who ate it sweat heavily; and when Xenophon recounts in Anabasis[6] that the Greek soldiers who had eaten honey on their way through Pontus had been severely poisoned, there is no reason to believe that it did not happen. On the other hand, it is rather embarrassing to find members of The Royal Society in London toward the end of the 17th century asking, in all seriousness, a traveler returned from India, Sir Philiberto Vernatti, whether the stories were true that "the Indians can so prepare the stupefying herb Datura, that they make it lie several days, months or years, according as they will have it, in a man's body, and at the end kill him without missing half an hour's time?"[7] As discussed in footnote 1 in the section on monkshood, Ambroise Paré had already pröved the impossibility of such a thing a hundred years beforehand.

What The Royal Society had called 'the stupefying herb Datura' was certainly *D. metel*. In its homeland this was used by the Thugs—worshippers of Kali, the goddess of fertility and death—partly to stupefy the human sacrifices which she demanded, partly so that the members of the sect could achieve the manic state which made it possible for them fearlessly to attack, stupefy and kill chance wayfarers—their preferred victims. It has been calculated that in the course of a

[5] Dioscorides, II, 103, p. 125.
[6] Anabasis, IV, viii, pp. 20–21.
[7] Bigelow's *American Medical Botany*, I–II, New York, 1817, 1st volume, pp. 21–22.

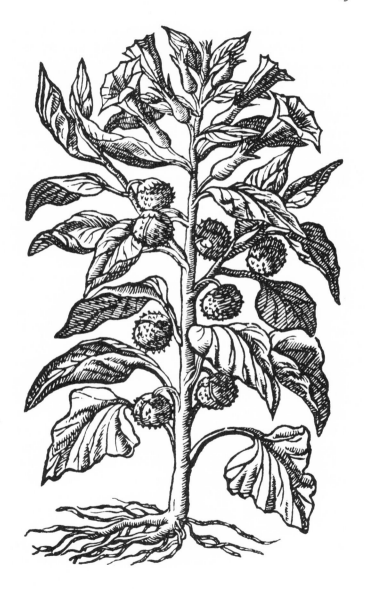

couple of centuries the Thugs succeeded in killing more than a hundred thousand people, before the Anglo-Indian authorities were able to crush them in the middle of the last century.

Many scholars identify the Hindu goddess Kali with the Greek goddess Io, who was believed by the maenads, the female worshippers of the Dionysian cult, to be the mother of Dionysus whom they worshipped, so it is supposed, in a state of ecstasy produced with the aid of thornapple juice. Strange as it may seem, a direct link can thus be traced between the Ancient Greek cult of Dionysus and the almost contemporary Indian Thug sect. The mythological stories of the visit of Dionysus and Io to India may be taken quite literally.

D. stramonium came to eastern North America with the very first European colonists—so early, that several botanists have been misled into believing that the herb was indigenous to America also. It appears that its bad reputation did not immediately accompany it across the Atlantic, for in 1676 it was used as an herb in soup by some soldiers encamped at Jamestown, Virginia. The results were that ". . . some of them eat plentifully of it, the Effect of which was a very pleasant Comedy; for they turn'd Fools upon it for several Days: One would blow up a Feather in the Air; another woul'd dart Straws at it with much Fury; and another stark naked was sitting in a Corner, like a Monkey, grinning and making Mows at them; a Fourth would fondly kiss, and paw his Companions, and snear in their Faces . . . In this frantick Condition they were confined, lest they should in their Folly destroy themselves; though it was thought that all their Actions were full of Innocence and good Nature . . . a Thousand such simple Tricks they play'd, and after Eleven Days, return'd to themselves again, not remembering anything that had pass'd."[8] [*Publisher's note:* Thornapple in the U.S. is commonly called Jimson weed, a name derived from its early Jamestown reference.]

In spite of being so dangerous, thornapple preparations were frequently used in love-philtres. They were, as an indignant German writer expressed it, "a tool of brothel-keepers, wicked seducers of girls, depraved courtesans and shameless lechers" when it was a case of making the victims lose their powers of resistance and become, against their will, sexually aroused, perhaps with subsequent loss of consciousness.

It was this kind of abuse that gained the plant the name 'love-will'. It was also called 'sorcerer's herb'. The name was apt, for the thornapple was among the herbs used by witches when they prepared their flying ointments.

Of all the magical herbs this is the easiest to cultivate. Once it is established in a place there is no need to fear that it will not automatically reappear the following year, but, coming from the south as it does, it prefers to grow in places that are sunny and protected from the wind.

[8] Robert Beverly's *History and Present State of Virginia* quoted by Heiser (1969), *Nightshades, the Paradoxical Plants*, p. 139. The possible existence of *Datura stramonium* in pre-Columbian America is discussed in Carrol L. Riley, J. Charles Kelley, Campbell W. Pennington and Robert L. Rands (editors): *Man Across the Sea—Problems of Pre-Columbian Contacts*, University of Texas Press, Austin and London, 1971.

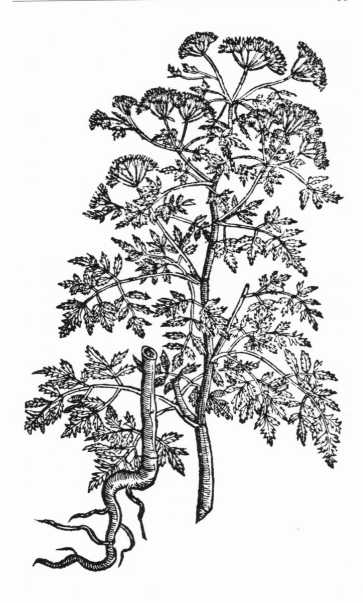

"My heart aches, and a drowsy numbness pains
My sense, as though of hemlock I had drunk . . ."

John Keats, "Ode to a Nightingale", 1820.

HEMLOCK

Conium maculatum, and WATER HEMLOCK, *Cicuta virosa.* When Socrates was given the cup of poison he said to the man who handed it to him: "You understand these matters. What should I do?" "Just empty the cup," the man answered, "then walk about until your legs feel heavy, and then lie down and the poison will act."

Socrates emptied the cup at a single draught. He walked around until he noticed heaviness in his legs and then laid down on his back. The man who handed the cup to him squeezed first his foot and then several places on the legs, gradually working upward to show the onlookers that Socrates had begun to grow cold and numb. "When the poison reaches the heart," he said, "Socrates will die." When the numbness reached his hips Socrates spoke his last words: "Crito, I owe a cock to Asclepius; will you remember to pay the debt?" Crito replied that he would and asked if there was anything else that should be done. But Socrates did not reply. Shortly afterwards a tremor passed through his limbs and his eyes became fixed. Crito saw this and closed his mouth and his eyes.

Thus died Socrates the Wise on an evening early in the year 399 B.C. It is probable that the poison cup contained hemlock juice mixed with laudanum and wine.[1] This mixture, according to Pliny,[2] was the usual means by which the Greeks did away with criminals condemned to death. Only the grossest malefactors were forced to drink aconitine, the monkshood poison, which caused a far more painful death. Plant poisons also played a role in other cultures beside the Greek. Among the Ancient Hebrews, who took life by stoning, and at the Roman crucifixions, the condemned sometimes received a pain-relieving narcotic drink before execution.

Even the most dangerous of the poisonous drugs can be useful if they are applied properly and the dosage is correct. Dioscorides writes that hemlock pounded in a mortar and smeared on the testicles "doth help wanton dreamers, and seed shedders," and then he states that hemlock plasters weaken the sexual parts. When used on women's breasts they dry up the milk, and they prevent virgins' breasts from becoming too large.[3] This last observation was, according to Pliny,[4] first

[1] Diogenes Laertius, who wrote at the beginning of the 3rd century A.D., states explicitly that the cup contained hemlock juice (II, 42 [1st vol., p. 173]), and the course of the poisoning—related here in a brief paraphrase of Plato's *Phaido*—indicates that he was right.
[2] Pliny, XXV, 151 (7th vol., p. 245).
[3] Dioscorides, IV, 79 (p. 478).
[4] Pliny, XXV, 154 (7th vol., p. 245).

made by Anaxilaus, and it is referred to two thousand years later by Simon Paulli in *Flora Danica*, where he writes that "girls' breasts that are rubbed with the juice of this herb do not grow thereafter, but remain properly small and do not change the size they are." This desire that the breasts "should not be too large under the translucent gauze" can, for us who live in the age of breast-worship, sound strange, but it was widely prevalent only a few decades ago.

It has been claimed that the use of hemlock to encourage chastity caused it to be brought to the North where it was not originally indigenous. It was used to subdue the lusts of the flesh in monks and nuns. Nor is there any doubt that it was cultivated in monastery gardens, for it is often found growing wild near monastery ruins, but it was certainly introduced long before the time of the monks. In any case it seems to have been a pre-Christian custom to let hemlock grow immediately outside the home, so that it could absorb any poison that might be about and thus keep the family hale and healthy. Probably the Vikings brought hemlock seeds back with them from their expeditions to the South and the West. They may have seen foreign surgeons giving local anaesthetics of hemlock juice to their patients before amputations, and they would quickly have realized how beneficial it would be to have this herb at hand in their homeland as well.

Hemlock and the related water hemlock, which grows wild in Denmark, belong to the large umbelliferous family. The herbs grow up to 125 centimeters tall and have large white umbels. The stalks are hollow and smooth, but as the stalk of the hemlock is also glistening and covered with scarlet spots, particularly on the lower part, it is easy to tell the difference between them. The second syllable of the Danish names, *skarntyde* and *gifttyde*, means 'nozzle', referring to their hollow stalks, whilst the first syllable of the name for hemlock, 'skarn', meaning dirt or refuse, refers perhaps to the places where the plant grows: rubbish dumps and so on near houses, outside city walls and on the shore, or, perhaps rather to the plant's bad smell. The first syllable of *gifttyde*, water hemlock, means poison.

In Greek antiquity the hemlocks were dedicated to the moon goddess Hecate, who protects and reigns over all that is hidden by darkness, and who was the mighty protectress and counselor of the witches, not only when they committed murder by poisoning but also when they occupied themselves with lesser arts or simply with low-down tricks such as chicken-stealing. "That thou may take birds with thy hands," it says in an old book of magic, "take any corn very well steeped in the dregs of wine and in the juice of Hemlock and cast it to the birds. Every bird that tasteth of it is made drunken and looseth her strength."[5]

The gypsies, who even nowadays are not welcome in the vicinity of henhouses, were apparently the witches' equals in this art and it is said that it was they especially who carried on the trade in hemlock seeds in the marketplaces outside the towns and that they, therefore, are responsible for the very wide distribution of hem-

[5] Attributed, without justification, to Albertus Magnus, the great scholastic philosopher of the 13th century. Cf. the introduction to Michael R. Best and Frank H. Brightman (eds.): *The Book of Secrets of Albertus Magnus*, Oxford, 1973.

lock. It is easy to give a dog a bad name and hang him; it is an accusation which cannot be proved—often seen in print but not therefore necessarily true.

In any case, it is beyond any doubt that in the time of the monks—long before the first gypsy had arrived in Denmark—hemlock was more widely distributed than it is now, because it was cultivated in every hospital or monastery garden. It was an important medical plant which, as already mentioned, was used, among other things, to keep the devotees of the cloistered life on the straight and narrow path of virtue, but which was also widely renowned for its ability to cure *ignis sacer*, St. Anthony's Fire, the result of ergot poisoning—one of the worst scourges of the Middle Ages.[6]

The more intensive cultivation of land and the use of chemical weed-killers have combined to make hemlock an increasingly rare plant. Water hemlock, on the other hand, is found frequently on lakeshores and on the banks of streams and brooks. It is by far the more dangerous of the two because its poisonous element, the spasm-producing cicutoxine, is more painful and, in the same dosage, more poisonous than the coniine in hemlock. Furthermore, when cooked the rootstock is almost indistinguishable in taste from celery or parsley root. In cases of poisoning the prognosis is bad: half of all cases of water hemlock poisoning prove fatal.

The witches used hemlock and water hemlock for

[6] On *ignis sacer* and ergot—or secale poisoning—cf. Vilhelm Møller-Christensen's *Mediaeval Medical Practice in Denmark* (Middelalderens Lægekunst i Danmark), Copenhagen, 1944, pp. 163–173 and Nielsen (1965), pp. 52–55.

much more than poisoning and chicken-stealing. These potent plants were included, among other things, in many flying ointments. Chemical experiments have proved that the poisons of the two hemlocks, especially coniine, taken in small doses or rubbed into the skin can produce the sensation of gliding through the air. In some flying ointment recipes other umbelliferae are mentioned, for example fool's parsley, *Aethusa cynapium*, which contains coniine in less concentrated form. This may have been used when the hemlocks were not available.

It was alleged that the natural development of sexual life within the bonds of matrimony, and thus pleasing to God, was an anathema to the Devil and the witches, and the witches were occasionally blamed for 'depriving a man of his secret member'. If there is anything other than the masculine fear of impotence behind this accusation, it is at least remotely conceivable that witches sometimes sneaked in to smear hemlock juice on men's genitals while they slept. People went to bed naked in the old days, so the feat could not have been too difficult to perform.

"No, no, go not to Lethe, neither twist
Wolf's-bane, tight-rooted, for its
poisonous wine . . ."

John Keats, "Ode on Melancholy", 1820.

MONKSHOOD

Aconitum napellus. A Greek myth tells that monkshood,
or wolfbane (wolf's poison), originated from the froth
that dripped from the jaws of the triple-headed Cerberus
when Hercules dragged him up from the underworld.
Saliva, either human or animal, was considered poisonous and the wilder the creature the more poisonous its
spittle. It is not surprising that this, of all the magical
herbs, must be considered the most dangerous, and
there is no lack of tragic examples of what can happen
if it is handled carelessly. Dr. William Turner writes
in his herbal of 1551 that some Frenchmen in Antwerp,
who mistook the shoots of this plant for masterwort,
all died, except for two, within 48 hours. Sir Francis
Bacon recounts in 1595 how he heard that only six or
seven flowers of this herb, mixed in a salad, killed a
French gentleman. An account in the 1636 edition of
John Gerard's herbal reads as though the incident were
still fresh in the memory: ". . . for when the leaves

hereof were by certain ignorant persons (in Antwerp) served up in sallads, all that did eat thereof were presently taken ill with most cruell symptomes and so died." In the 18th century Dr. John Hill wrote in his *British Herbal* of "five persons who eat the root of it, through a mistake, in their food at Antwerp, and all died."

Monkshood is an erect and beautiful plant which may grow up to one-and-a-half meters tall. It has petiolate, deeply divided, dark green leaves and many blossoms which are gathered in a cluster toward the top of the stalk. The petals of the flowers are completely hidden by the five petal-like, violet-blue sepals, of which the uppermost, the 'monkshood', is broader than it is long. All parts of the plant—including the seeds and the thick, knobby rootstock—are poisonous.

Many hunting cultures, from the Ainus in the East to the Irish in the West, have used aconitine as arrow poison. In this connection it is interesting to recall Dr. Margaret Murray's theory that the elf-people, who played such a large role in European folklore, were in reality aborigines who had been driven back from fertile regions to the wastelands and mountains. 'Elf-bolts', so-called, were originally poison arrowheads. It has been proved that the people of the Early Stone Age in Europe were familiar with the use of poison arrows. The poison must certainly have been the fast-acting aconitine rather than hemlock poison, as supposed by Dr. Murray and others, as the latter works too slowly to be effective.

Murder and attempted murder by poison were so common in antiquity and the Middle Ages that princes and great men could never feel certain of surviving from one meal to the next. The fear and uncertainty were increased by the fact that far greater powers were ascribed to the concoctors of poison than they actually possessed. Theophrastus, Aristotle's pupil, recounts that aconitine can be prepared so that death does not occur for two, three or six months, or until one or two years have elapsed![1] However, this poison was also insidious in another way. A legend about this, which is, however, demonstrably untrue, tells how Aristotle saved the life of Alexander the Great during his Indian campaign.

An Indian prince, who feared that Alexander would seize his kingdom, had hatched out a devilish scheme to put him out of the way. "Bring me the most beautiful girl in the whole of my kingdom," he said to his servants, and when they had fulfilled his demand, he made the young lady take a daily increased dose of aconitine. After a few weeks she was completely saturated with the poison, but because of the gradual habituation she continued in the best of health and looked, if possible, even lovelier than before. Then the wicked prince had her arrayed in a costly sari and adorned with precious jewelry, after which he dispatched her as a gift to Alexander. It was absolutely certain that the Macedonian would die if he so much as kissed or caressed her. But that was not the way it worked out. When she arrived at the Greek camp it was the sage Aristotle who saw her first and, being so

[1] Theophrastus, II, pp. 299–300. This cock-and-bull story was finally scotched by Ambroise Paré some nineteen hundred years later, but as we have seen in the section on *Datura stramonium*, it was still cropping up as late as the end of the 17th century.

clever, he could see immediately that it was poison and not the light of love that made the Indian beauty's eyes shine so soulfully and enchantingly—and Alexander was saved![2]

Unfortunately, we now know that Aristotle never took part in the Indian campaign at all. As far as the poisoned damsel is concerned, she would have been quite harmless; it is perhaps possible to develop a tolerance for doses of aconitine so large that they would be immediately fatal to anyone not habituated to the drug, but just as it is impossible to die from intimate contact with a nicotine-saturated tobacco smoker, it is equally impossible to die from intercourse with aconitine-saturated beauties. Only they did not know that in those days.

A more probable and at the same time more macabre story is to be found in Pliny's *Natural History,* where he recounts that Calpurnius Bestia, a Roman Bluebeard, murdered one wife after another by smearing their sexual parts with aconitine while they were asleep.[3]

The most famous Roman murder mystery, however, came about in the year 54 A.D. when the Emperor Claudius died in mysterious circumstances. The then contemporary historian Tacitus accused Julia Agrippina, Claudius' Empress, of having had him done away with, so her son by a previous marriage, Nero, could ascend the throne.[4] The first attempt is said to

[2] Cf. Fr. Moth's *Aristotelessagnet eller Elskovs Magt,* Copenhagen, 1916, p. 153 ff. In German there is Wilhelm Hertz's *Die Sage vom Giftmädchen,* Berlin, 1905, and in English N. M. Penzer's *Poison-Damsels and Other Essays in Folklore and Anthropology,* London, 1952.

[3] Pliny, XXVII, 4 (7th vol., p. 391).

have been made with a dish of poisonous mushrooms, but the old Emperor only suffered violent nausea. Then aconitine was spread on the feather with which his throat was tickled to produce vomiting, to free him of whatever might have made him ill. It worked, and Nero became Emperor. The actual poisoner, Locusta, who in collusion with Claudius' own personal physician, Stertinius Xenophon,[5] had seen to the purely practical side, was given other exciting jobs, including the poisoning of Britannicus, Claudius' son, who had been Nero's co-Emperor.

In the Middle Ages monkshood was sometimes

> ". . . prepaired in monkish cell
> To thin the scarlet conclave of old men",

and even a Pope, Adrian VI, is said to have been poisoned by it. The Prophet Mohammed also almost became a victim, so it is said at least. Zeinab, a young Jewish girl whose father and brother the Prophet had murdered, disguised herself as a servant girl, succeeded in getting into his house and offered him a piece of meat prepared with aconitine. But Mohammed politely offered it to a guest who ate it and died on the spot. There was great indignation and Zeinab, who had behaved as treacherously as the horrid animal in the rhyme:

---

[4] *The Annals of Tacitus*, XII, pp. 66–67.
[5] His name, with the addition 'philoneron', that is, 'Nero's friend', may still be read on a statue pediment which is to be found in the sanctuary of Asclepius on the Island of Cos in the Aegean Sea.

"Cet animal est très méchant,
Quand on l'attaque il se défend!"

was handed over to the guest's relations and was stoned
to death.[6] This completely unsubstantiated story is
probably the original source of the unfounded and
malicious reputation as poisoners which hung over the
heads of the Jews throughout the Middle Ages. As
recently as 1942 the story of Zeinab was revived by the
Nazis, dusted off and retold, with bows and bells on it,
in Goebbel's propaganda broadcasts to Arab countries.

A wise man once said that the history of poisonous
plants is also the history of medicines. During the First
World War the Central Powers used aconitine as a
substitute for failing reserves of morphine. The poison
is still used here and there as a heart stimulant in
homoeopathic medicine, but on the whole it may be
said that physicians have been afraid of it. They have
most often been in agreement with the physician
Leonard Fuchs, who wrote in 1543 that "although
Dioscorides states that aconitine can be used externally
against soreness of the eyes, it is wisest to leave such
dangerous herbs alone."[7] We must agree with him, for
whoever is poisoned by aconitine is in danger; there
was—and is today—no effective antidote. Fortunately,
the poison breaks down quickly and if the respiration
of the poisoned person can be kept going artificially
during the decomposition process, the danger is over.

There is a large number of *Aconitum* species, but

[6] More detailed versions are given in Mathison (1958), p. 140 and
Bergmark (1967), p. 23.
[7] Fuchs (1543), Chap. XXX.

none of them grow wild in Denmark. *Aconitum septentrionale* is found in Norway and Sweden, and as *A. napellus* came early to Denmark with the monks we may assume that the Scandinavian witches knew either one or both of the species and used them in the flying ointments with which they rubbed themselves before the sabbat journeys. Unfortunately, monkshood poison was also used for another, less innocent purpose: it was put into love-philtres, and as the poison content can vary considerably from plant to plant, the dosage was difficult to calculate, and it could happen that the victim who was to be charmed went mad or died instead.

One would think that most garden owners would refuse to have such a dangerous poisonous plant as *A. napellus* growing in their flower-beds. Not so! It is, in fact, a very common ornamental plant in Danish gardens. It may be that it has sneaked in under cover-names: 'chariot of Venus', 'friar's cap', 'king's coach', or 'monkshood'. (The common Danish name is *storm-hat,* which is a kind of helmet known in English as a morion.) Whatever it is called, you should be very careful, dear reader. Otherwise you may suffer the same fate as an entire family who recently died a painful death somewhere in Europe (Antwerp, perhaps?) after eating a few monkshood leaves added by mistake into the vegetables accompanying a roast canard.

> *"He little knows the Devil who does*
> *not believe that witches and wizards*
> *can be borne through the air at*
> *wondrous speed to far distant places*
> *and there hold revels, dances and*
> *suchlike with folk of the same type."*

Bishop Jesper Brochmand,
Systema universæ theologiæ,
1633.

THE WITCHES' FLYING OINTMENTS

Even the witches of antiquity could fly. We know this from, among others, Apuleius, whose hero Lucius got into terrible trouble when he was trying to imitate the witch Pamphilë on whom he had spied while she smeared herself with ointment and disappeared over the rooftops in the guise of an owl. Lucius wanted to repeat Pamphilë's act but dipped his hand in the wrong jar, which the maidservant, in her hurry, had given him by mistake. Anointing himself, Lucius was changed, not into an owl, but into *The Golden Ass*. Rarely, however, did things go as badly as this. Classical literature —for example Ovid's *Metamorphoses* and Petronius' *Satyricon*—contains many accounts in which the preparations and the flights themselves went off without the least mishap. The belief that witches could appear in the forms of owls was also very much alive in the

Middle Ages. The Italian language has preserved a curious memento of this fact: *strega*, the current term for a witch, is, through the mediæval Latin *striga*, derived from the classical Latin *strix*, an owl.

The Church in the Middle Ages seems originally to have rejected this superstition. In any case, what is known as the *Canon episcopi*[1] contains an instruction to Bishops to keep an eye open for "certain women who, tricked by the Devil, imagine that in the night-time, riding on certain animals, they fly a great distance together with the heathen goddess Diana, with Herodias and with bands of other women." But the clerical authorities changed their opinion at the beginning of the 15th Century. After the annihilation of the heretical sects, the Church started in earnest its fight against the European community of witches. Every allegation that could cast a suspicious light on witches was accepted without reservation, and the belief that they could fly with the aid of the Devil became, during the following centuries, almost a dogma which only a few—least of all the witches themselves—dared to doubt.

With regard to the witches' point of view, the Dominican Bartholomæus de Spina (1465–1546) tells in his *Tractatus de strigibus sive maleficis*, 1525, a story related by an acquaintance of his, the physician Augustus de Turre of Bergamo. As a young man he had stud-

---

[1] The account which follows is mainly based on Soldan-Heppe (1880), Kiesewetter (1895) and Peuckert (1960) and (1967), and also Robbins (1959). The quotation from *Canon episcopi* is translated from Soldan-Heppe, I, p. 107. The two rabid witch-hunters who wrote *Malleus maleficarum* maintained that precisely this passage "has been intolerably harmful to the Holy Church."

ied in Pavia and one evening he came home so late to his lodgings that nobody opened the door or answered his knocking. At last he climbed onto a balcony on the first floor and got into the house through a window. He at once looked for the maidservant to reprimand her, but found her lying unconscious and motionless on the floor of her room. When they met the next morning he tried to question her about the matter, but she only replied that she had been 'on a journey'.

Elsewhere in the same work de Spina relates that a notary from Lugano, unable to find his wife one morning, searched for her all over the estate where they lived and finally found her lying unconscious, naked and dirty in a corner of the pigsty. He immediately understood that she was a witch and wanted to kill her on the spot, but had second thoughts. When, a little later, she regained consciousness and saw how agitated he was she fell on her knees before him and confessed that during the night she had been 'on a journey'.

Partly on the flimsy basis of reality afforded by these and similar stories, the witch-hunters gradually built up the picture of the sabbat which we know now from countless books and illustrations. The witches are 'on a journey' and come to the Brocken, where they are received by the Devil in his own high person. The witch novices—often children or young people—immediately seal a pact with him and are marked by him, and the old witches kiss him on the backside as a sign of continued allegiance. When these rituals are over there is dancing and feasting, but the food and drink is so-so; it is often bad or inedible. During the dancing and feasting the Devil has intercourse with everyone present, an unpleasant or painful experience because

his member is ice-cold and extremely large. The revels culminate in an orgy with witches and devils, young and old, copulating indiscriminately. And to these stereotyped accounts is sometimes added the observation that before their sabbat journeys the witches smeared themselves with an ointment which they had either obtained from the Devil or which they themselves had prepared according to his directions.

Many stories were told about this mysterious ointment. *Malleus maleficarum* contains the story of a witch who confessed under examination that "we set our snares especially for unbaptized infants, but also for those who have been baptized but are not protected by the sign of the cross or prayers . . . and kill them through conjurations in the cradle, or even when they are sleeping at their parents' side so that they assume afterwards that they were accidentally smothered or died from some other natural cause. Afterwards we remove them secretly from their graves and cook them in a cauldron until the flesh is boiled away from the bones to make, partly a broth which can well be drunk, and partly, from the more solid bits, an ointment which can be used to help us in our arts, pleasures and journeyings. The broth we put into a bottle or wineskin and whoever drinks of it while observing certain rites immediately gains great wisdom and becomes a leader in our sect."[2]

Many scholars who, in the last half of the 16th century and onwards, interested themselves in flying ointments were unsatisfied with this simple and straightforward explanation. Sir Francis Bacon had perhaps the above quotation in mind when in 1626, shortly before his

[2]*Malleus*, Part II, Qn. 1, Ch. 2.

death, he wrote: "The ointment that witches use, is
reported to be made of the fat of children digged out of
their graves; of the juices of smallage, wolf-bane, and
cinquefoil, mingled with the meal of fine wheat. But
I suppose, that the soporiferous medicines are likeliest
to do it; which are henbane, hemlock, mandrake,
moonshade, tobacco, opium, saffron, poplar-leaves,
etc."[3] We shall see that he was only partly right. His
Italian contemporary, Doctor Giambattista della Porta,
(1538–1615) had described in his most important
work, *Magia naturalis,* 1589, a number of ointments
which all contained 'the soporiferous medicines' opium,
henbane, hemlock and others, but also the fat of children! The *Malleus* witch, who had suppressed the
active ingredients of her ointment, had not lied about
child fat: it often formed part of the ointment, sometimes euphemistically referred to as *ein gewisses Fleisch*
(a certain flesh). Bat's blood, the viper and the toad
also appear in the ointments, but only the last-named,
which contains the poison bufotenine, is chemically
active.

Quite a large number of flying ointment recipes are
known from the time of witches, but only comparatively few of them are complete. Nearly all of them
lack precise specifications as to the proportions in
which the various ingredients should be used, and
some contain only inactive or slightly active substances
which could certainly not have taken any witch far on
'a journey'. If we disregard the recipes which are too
incomplete, some sixteen are left which are comparatively reliable. These are found in works such as the

---

[3]*Sylva Sylvarum,* Cent. X, Par. 975.

above by della Porta, in *De praestigiis daemonum, et cantationibus, ac ueneficiis* of 1536 by Doctor Johann Weyer (1515–1586), in *De subtilitate rerum* of 1550 by Gerolamo Cardano (1501–1576) and in *De la Lycanthropie, Transformation, et Extase des Sorciers* of 1615 by Jean de Nynauld. It is mainly the recipes from these works which have been tested in modern times by the historians Karl Kiesewetter, Will-Erich Peuckert and others. It is the ingredients—or the presumed ingredients—from a selection of sixteen of these authors' recipes which are given in the following list, the figure on the right showing the number of recipes in which the individual ingredients are included.

Plant ingredients

1. Water Hemlock, *Cicuta virosa*   5
2. Hemlock, *Conium maculatum*   2
3. Celery, *Apium spp.*   3
4. "Eleoselinum", which can be taken to mean:
   a. Wild Celery, *Apium graveolens*
   b. Parsley, *Petroselinum spp.*
   c. Parsnip, *Pastinaca spp.*
   d. Fool's Parsley, *Aethusa cynapium*
   e. Water Hemlock, *Cicuta virosa*   3
5. "Sium", which can be taken to mean:
   a. Water Parsnip, *Sium spp.*
   b. Speedwell, *Veronica spp.*
   c. Watercress, *Nasturtium officinale*
   d. Water Hemlock, *Cicuta virosa*   2
6. Sweet Flag, *Acorus calamus*   3
7. Yellow Flag, *Iris pseudacorus*   2
8. Water-lily, either:

	a. White Water-lily, *Nymphaea alba,* or	
	b. Yellow Water-lily, *Nuphar luteum*	1
9.	Creeping Cinquefoil, *Potentilla reptans*	8
10.	Tormentil, *Potentilla erecta*	1
11.	Monkshood, *Aconitum napellus*	7
12.	Poppy, *Papaver spp.*	4
13.	Deadly Nightshade, *Atropa belladonna*	8
14.	Henbane, *Hyoscyamus niger*	3
15.	Black Nightshade, *Solanum nigrum*	2
16.	Mandrake, *Mandragora officinarum*	1
17.	Thornapple, *Datura stramonium*	1
18.	Spurge, *Euphorbia sp.*	1
19.	Darnel, *Lolium temulentum*	3
20.	Lettuce, *Lactuca spp.*	2
21.	Purslane, *Portulaca sp.*	1
22.	Poplar, *Populus spp.*	4
23.	Oil	4
24.	Incense	1
25.	Soot	7

Animal ingredients[4]

1.	Child's fat	6
2.	Bat's blood	5

Identification of the plants. We have presented a clear and straightforward list of well-known plants, but for the many experts whom we have to thank for these

---

[4] As far as is known, child's fat and bat's blood are chemically inactive substances which need not be discussed in further detail in a book on witches' herbs. The interested reader is referred to Hovorka u. Kronfeld (1908–09) where these and other animal ointment ingredients are described.

identifications the work has not been easy, nor can we always be quite certain of our facts. Uncertainty may exist even over the generic names, and for many of the herbs an exact determination of the species is not possible.

As regards 1. Water hemlock and 2. Hemlock, it is known that in former times a distinction was definitely made between them, but the same pharmacological properties were attributed to both of them and their botanical names were interchanged according to fancy. 3. Celery is possibly wild celery, *Apium graveolens,* but the designation 'Apium' is sometimes synonymous with 5. 'Sium' which, as is shown in the list, can be four different plants but is most often water parsnip. 4. 'Eleoselinum' is most often a celery but, as shown, the name is used to denote at least four other plants. 6. Sweet flag, originating from India, has the peculiarity that it is not known for certain whether it came to Europe during the first half of the 16th Century or much earlier,[5] and when it occurs in an ointment, 7. Yellow flag may sometimes have been meant. The possibility of confusion between 9. Creeping cinquefoil and 10. Tormentil cannot be excluded. 8. Waterlily is, as indicated, either the white or the yellow water-lily. 11. Monkshood is probably always a certain identification, but the possibility of confusion with the thora buttercup, *Ranunculus Thora,* whose pre-Linnean name was *Aconitum pardalianches,* can presumably not be ruled out. 12. Poppy can be either the opium poppy, *Papaver somniferum,* or the corn poppy, *Papaver rhoeas*—in one of the recipes with which we are con-

[5] Cf. Nielsen (1965), p. 92.

cerned here, both kinds are included. 13. Deadly nightshade is certain enough, but the Linnean generic name,
Atropa, was sometimes used for mandrake, so confusion is possible. Deadly nightshade can also presumably be confused with certain nightshades with which
it once shared the generic name *Solanum.* 14. Henbane
can always be identified with certainty. For 15. Black
nightshade and 16. Mandrake the same qualifications
apply as those mentioned for deadly nightshade. With
regard to 17. Thornapple, it may be noted that there
was a short period (almost certainly only during the
18th century) when *Datura stramonium* was understood
to refer, not to the thornapple, but sometimes to holly,
Ilex aquifolium, as well as to garden balsam, *Balsamina
hortensis.* There is no doubt about 19. Darnel but, as
shown, the species of 18. Spurge cannot be determined,
and the same applies to 20. Lettuce, which may be garden lettuce, *Lactuca sativa,* but is more often poison
lettuce, *L. virosa,* or one of the other wild species. The
species of 21. Purslane cannot be determined either,
and with regard to 22. Poplar, it is possible that sometimes there was no question of leaves or shoots from
poplar trees, but in fact of leaves from a species of mallow, *Malva sp.,* which in older German went under the
name of *Pappel* or *Poppel* (which are also the German
names for poplar) and which was a witch's herb. 23.
Oils can be pressed from beans and other plants but in
some recipes the designation is certainly a euphemism
for child's fat. 24. Incense can be made from juniper,
Juniperus spp., which was also regarded by the witches
as a holy bush and had once been dedicated to the god
Thor. 25. Soot is just simply soot.

The effects of the plant substances. The well-known historian of witchcraft and magic Dr. Karl Kiesewetter—one of the first to experiment with witches' ointments in modern times—died of poisoning after one of his experiments. What the poison was is not known, but if we look back at the list of the plants we will find several which, used internally, are fatal in a sufficiently high dosage, and some—for instance monkshood—which can be deadly dangerous applied externally. From this one might get the impression that the witches risked their lives every time they smeared themselves with the ointments, but there is no evidence that they ever ran into trouble. The reason for this is undoubtedly that the preparation of the ointment was entrusted only to those witches who knew their plants so well that any risk was ruled out in advance.

We shall not go further into the chemical components of the ointment herbs or the composition of these components beyond what has been said in the foregoing chapters—this seems unnecessary as information on the subject is readily available in pharmacological handbooks. It is sufficient to say that a great majority of the herbs contain chemically active substances of various kinds. Used separately, the plants can have a muscle-relaxing, soothing or soporific effect, and some of these latter—for instance poppy or thornapple—are at the same time hallucinatory. Some of the herbs had a reputation as aphrodisiacs in olden times. That was the case, according to Peuckert (1960), with celery and parsley, but it applies also to other umbelliferous plants, particularly if, like the wild carrot, *Daucus carota*, they were equipped with a well-developed, aromatic tap-root. Some of the umbelliferous plants

designated as 'Eleoselinum' and 'Sium' belong in this category, as well as yellow flag and spurge, both of which were reputed to produce 'lust and lechery'. But spurge contains a caustic, milky juice which may conceivably have effected the absorption of the ointment through the skin. Plants containing milky juice—and there are several on the list—were considered to have a magically strengthening effect on women in particular, and several of them also contain substances which have a soothing and muscle-relaxing effect. Sweet flag has also been used as an aphrodisiac, but whether that was the reason for including it in the ointments is doubtful. One would have thought that there were enough aphrodisiacs already, but they may all have been necessary to counterbalance the two water-lilies which, according to the 1923 edition of Henrik Smid, "completely extinguish the sensual lusts which are incorporated in every human being." Tormentil and creeping cinquefoil were believed to increase night vision. The latter and mallow were fivefold herbs and therefore magical. What Darnel, the Biblical tare, and Shakespeare's "Darnel, and all the idle weeds that grow in our sustaining corn" was doing in the ointments is not immediately obvious. The seeds are poisonous and cause dizziness. Large doses cause paralysis, and it was possibly this effect that was intended. Lettuce, particularly poison lettuce, has to a milder degree the same effects as the poppy and is said to give pleasant dreams. Purslane "subdues the excessive urge for copulation or the Natural Act, and it prevents the dreams one has about such natural dalliance," says Simon Paulli. It is hard to say what its role was as an ingredient of the ointment. The black poplar's leaves were included among Sir Francis Bacon's 'soporific drugs', and a fragrant ointment was made of its fresh buds.

Most researchers agree that the individual chemical ingredients of the plants are mainly responsible for the different phases of the sabbat experience. "The witches' ointments are perhaps therefore particularly interesting psychopharmacologically," says Leuner (1968), p. 90, "because we are evidently dealing here with the world's only known technique for producing toxic ecstasy in which specific components of the experience are brought about through the art of psychopharmacological composition."

This art was fully understood by the witches. They knew that every single chemical component of the ointment affected the other materials through the working of what is now called catalysis. They understood how to use precisely those herbs which in exactly measured doses formed the chemical combination which gave the ointment the desired effects. Soldan, even in his time, raised the question of whether ointments existed which necessarily had the same effects on all who used them. For the purpose of the witches' ride and the witches' sabbat, there is every indication that such ointments did exist. But the witches took the art—the correct composition of the ointments—with them to the grave, or, if one will, to the stake, since today not a single ointment recipe is known of which it can be said that the individual components are definitely identified, that the chemical contents of all the ingredients are explained, or that the exact dosage of each component is clearly established.

Contemporary experiments which attempt to test the witches' ointments have consequently only a very limited validity. But everyone who has tried to learn the secret of the ointments has been confronted with another, equally insurmountable difficulty, which Wagner (1970), among others, points out: that no one alive today is in a position to know what the witches felt and thought when they smeared themselves with the ointment and set out 'on a journey'. The basic situation, cultural and physical as well as psychic, can never be the same.[6] This is the reason why Kiesewetter, Peuckert and other researchers who experiment on themselves experience a sabbat which is hardly distinguishable from the caricature sketched here. "We

[6] Many a mediæval witch must have suffered to some degree from ergot poisoning, or 'St. Anthony's Fire.' Ergot poisoning was occasionally epidemic and at all times endemic to those parts of Europe where rye bread was the staff of life. This is a factor which seems to have been ignored by modern experimenters.

experienced in dreams first wild and yet restricted
flights, and then chaotic revels, like the wild tumult of
an annual fairground, and finally progressed to erotic
licentiousness," relates Peuckert (1967) about an experiment on himself with one of della Porta's ointments, carried out in about 1927 together with one
of his friends.

If the sabbat journeys did take place—and historical
and folkloric research seem to confirm that they did—
and if we cannot imagine that Europe's witches in their
thousands at certain times of the year and of their own
free will (and at the risk of torture, the stake and eternal
damnation) rubbed themselves with ointment and
went 'on a journey' simply to experience scenes full of
horror and ghastliness, then we must assume that the
reality of the sabbats was different from what we have
always been told. If we look more closely at the witches'
confessions we are struck by the fact that the sabbat is
described in terms which may vary but which nearly
always give the same general picture. It has been said
that it was the examining judges' own fantastic ideas
of the sabbat that find expression here through the
attempts of the mistreated witches to echo their tor-
turers' words. But it is also conceivable that the identical confessions were a put-up job. Parodies, plausible
to contemporary eyes, were the means by which the
witches were able, to the bitter end, to protect the
mysteries of the sabbat and of the witches' religion.

This assumption is strengthened by the fact that we
can see from the reports of the trials that the witches'
contemporary descriptions of the sabbat vary only—
but in these cases quite drastically—when it is children
or young people who are being examined. A young

French witch tells the court that "the sabbat is the true paradise, where greater delights are to be found than one can describe. Those who go there find the time too short for all the happiness and pleasure they enjoy, so that they leave it with sorrow and a longing to come again." Another young witch declares that the devil dominates her will and heart to such an extent that she will probably never again fancy anyone else, and that the joys of the sabbat were only a foretaste of far greater glory. A third, the sixteen-year-old Scots girl Gillie Duncan, describes the sabbat as an idyllic picnic in the moonlight, almost what one might expect if one followed the children's call:

> *"Boys and girls come out to play*
> *The moon doth shine as bright as day!"*

One might imagine that these young people had either not come under a vow of silence and had not been instructed by their older fellow witches what story they should tell in such a situation, or perhaps they had simply been unable to keep silent about the truth and had confessed as much under examination as they knew.[7]

---

[7] "A boy comes to Tromskirke together with his mother, the one on a baker's shovel, the other on a broomstick; there was a black man who looked gentle, talked in a friendly way to everybody, poured wine out of a bottle, and taught the people a lot of things." (E. T. Kristensen, *Jyske Folkeminder*, (Jutland's Folklore) VII, 262.446 ff.). This folkloric record is also a reminiscence of a child's account of a sabbat. Another striking example is found in Fr. Hammerich's "Skandinaviske Reiseminder" ("Memories of Scandinavian Travels") in *Brage og Ydun* (1839) pp. 369–81.

Was the sabbat a dream or reality? The English phar-macologist A. C. Clark, who analysed some of the oint-ment recipes, wrote in 1921 that "irregular action of the heart in a person falling asleep produces the well known sensation of suddenly falling through space, and it seems quite possible that the combination of a delirifacient like belladonna with a drug producing irregular action of the heart like aconite might produce the sensation of flying."[8] Dr. Clark's theory could be re-examined by any pharmacologist today with the same result, but it does not really tell us more than we know after reading about de Spina's two witches on their 'journeys'.

In *Vatnsdaela Saga* one can read an account of the magical journeys of the Norwegian Lapps to distant regions to find out how things were going on there. The witches claimed that they took part in the sabbat in the spirit while their temporarily inanimate bodies stayed at home. Spiritualists have long claimed that what they call man's astral body can undertake jour-neys while the physical body stays where it is—accounts of magical journeys come to us from all religions, from all ages and from all parts of the world, and the phe-nomenon that is described seems to be basically the same, regardless of the era or culture from which it originates.

The witches' ride and sabbat are generally considered today as phenomena which had no actual reality. With the aid of the ointment the witches came into contact with a supernatural world, heard voices and saw phan-

[8] In an Appendix to Murray's *The Witch-Cult in Western Europe* (1921).

toms, and afterwards could not grasp—wrapped in black superstition as they were—that the whole thing had been a narcotic dream. Among scientific pioneers this view of the matter was already current in the 1600s and the difficulty in abandoning this view today arises mainly from the fact that in such a case one would have to accept what one had previously rejected—the old dualistic conception that the soul and body are separate, interacting entities, and that the soul is independent of the brain and can exist and function without it. But we live in a world which has seen one scientific law after another totter or be completely overthrown, and the most recent parapsychological research has shown that our conceptions of the life of the soul in relation to the brain are too inadequate to explain a whole series of phenomena, and must therefore be revised. It would not be surprising if such a revision led to our having in the future to accept the witches' ride and the witches' sabbat as phenomena which really took place, even if on a plane which we have not so far been able to explore.

THE WITCHES' BREW IN MACBETH.

The great poet Shakespeare shows in all his plays a thorough knowledge of the superstitious conception of the world by his contemporaries. When we read the tragedy of Macbeth we can be certain that the description of the three witches and their brews reflects what the contemporary man in the street imagined that witches put in their brews:

> *"Eye of newt, and toe of frog,*
> *Wool of bat, and tongue of dog,*
> *Adder's fork, and blind-worm's sting,*
> *Lizard's leg and howlet's wing—"*

and one may easily get the impression that all these curious ingredients—apparently all of animal origin—are pure imagination on Shakespeare's part.

This is not the case.

Two of them, 'tongue of dog' and 'adder's fork', are plants. The former, the *Cynoglossum officinale*, is hound's-tongue, and the latter is the fern *Ophioglossum vulgatum*, which is adder's-tongue. Real 'dispensing' witches probably had no great use for them, but they were both highly regarded as medicinal plants, and popular belief ascribed magical powers to them. To enter unnoticed into a house guarded by dogs one should strew leaves of hound's-tongue on the ground in front of it, for as soon as the dogs tread on the leaves they are unable either to bark or to bite. Shakespeare knew this tradition but, sceptical as he was, he must surely have suspected that it was the disgustingly nauseous smell of the plant—particularly of the flowers—which made the dogs react in such an abnormal manner. He was also aware of the fact that doctors used the root of hound's-tongue, which contains the alkaloid cynoglossine, together with parts of two really dangerous witches' herbs, henbane seeds and the milky juice of the opium poppy, to produce an ancient and highly esteemed cough cure, cynogloss pills, which can still be bought from both English and Danish chemists.

All ferns had an aura of mysticism, and the little adder's-tongue, doubtless because of its distinctive shaft with two rows of sporangia, was strongly suspected of bearing the magic fern seeds.

A little further on in the text we read that the three witches cast 'scale of dragon' and 'tooth of wolf' into the magical broth as well as

"*Witch's mummy, maw and gulf
Of the ravin'd salt-sea shark,*

Root of hemlock digg'd i' th' dark,
Liver of blaspheming Jew,
Gall of goat, and slips of yew
Sliver'd in the moon's eclipse,
Nose of Turk, and Tartar's lips,
Finger of birth-strangled babe
Ditch-deliver'd by a drab—"

Was 'scale of dragon' a plant? The possibility has been discussed, but it is also conceivable that Shakespeare had Medea's team of dragons in mind, for it is known

that he was familiar with Ovid's *Metamorphoses* and had read both the original and Arthur Golding's English translation. There is no doubt about 'tooth of wolf'—this is our old friend monkshood, here hiding under one of its cover-names.

But even if three, or perhaps four, of the ingredients (in addition to hemlock and 'slips of yew'—*Taxus baccata*) prove, on closer inspection, to be plants, there are still some pretty strange things left in the pot. As far as these are concerned, they are all, without exception, associated with paganism or the forces of evil: The newt, toad, lizard and blind-worm are, like the adder and all other reptiles, made by the Evil One; the owl and the bat also; the shark, goat and tiger are, each in their own way, creatures of the devil; Jews, Tartars and Turks are unbaptized and therefore destined to go to hell; even the little mite that was strangled without baptism had, according to the strict theologians, to spend eternity in hell, although the majority believed that a better future was in store for the little soul: *Limbus puerorum*, a special place for unbaptized children, equidistant from heaven and hell.

The folklorist Svend Grundtvig once said that superstition has its own natural laws, and it must certainly be admitted that Shakespeare followed these very closely.

BIBLIOGRAPHY

Aelian
    On the Characteristics of Animals Translated
    by A. F. Scolfield. Loeb Classical Library, I–III,
    London, 1958–59.
Albertus Magnus
    Book of Minerals Translated by Dorothy
    Wyckoff. Oxford, 1967.
    The Book of Secrets of Albertus Magnus Edited
    by Michael R. Best and Frank H. Brightman.
    Oxford, 1973.
Apollonius Rhodius
    Argonautica Translated by R. C. Seaton. Loeb
    Classical Library, London, 1912.
Arber, Agnes
    Herbals, Their Origin and Evolution, 2nd Edition Cambridge, 1938.
Bacon, Sir Francis
    The Works of Francis Bacon, I–V London,
    1765.

Baroja, Julio Caro
   Die Hexen und ihre Welt   Stuttgart, 1967.
Bergmark, Matts
   Vellyst or Smerte   Translated by Ole Hemming-
   sen, Danish edition prepared by Otto Lindemark.
   Copenhagen, 1967.
Bock, Hieronymus
   *New Kreutterbuch von underscheydt, würckung
   und namen der kreütter so in Teutschen Landen
   wachen*   Strassburg, 1539 and 1551.
Brunnfeltz, Otho
   Kontrafayt Kreuterbuch . . .   Strassburg, 1532,
   photographic reprint.
Clark, Anne
   Beasts and Bawdy   London, 1975.
Culpeper, Nicholas
   English Physician Enlarged . . .   London,
   1653. Modern reprint, London, no date.
Diogenes Laertius
   Lives of Eminent Philosophers   Translated by
   R. D. Hicks. Loeb Classical Library, I–II, Lon-
   don, 1925.
Dioscorides
   The Greek Herbal   Translated by John Good-
   yer, 1655. Edited by Robert T. Gunther. London,
   1933. Reprinted 1968.
Fuchs, Leonhard
   New Kreüterbuch . . .   Basel, 1543, photo-
   graphic reprint.
Gerard, John
   see Woodward, Marcus
Gimbutas, Marija
   The Gods and Goddesses of Old Europe   Lon-
   don, 1974.

Heiberg, J. L.
Af Læ gemidlernes Historie i den Classiske Oldtid Copenhagen, 1917.
Heiser, Charles B.
Nightshades, the Paradoxical Plants San Francisco, 1969.
Heppe, Heinrich
see Soldan-Heppe
Hovorka, O. von and Kronfeld A.
Vergleichende Volksmedizin I–II Stuttgart, 1908–09.
Josephus Flavius
Works Translated by H. Thackeray, R. Marcus, Allen Wikgren and L. H. Feldman. Loeb Classical Library, I–IX, London, 1926–65.
Kiesewetter, Karl
Geschichte des Neueren Occultismus Leipzig, 1892.
Die Geheimwissenschaften Leipzig, 1895.
Kramer, Heinrich and Sprenger, James
Malleus malleficarum 1486.
Malleus maleficarum Translated from Latin by Montague Summers. London, 1928. Reprinted 1971.
Kronfeld, A. and Hovorka, C. von
see Hovorka, C. von and Kronfeld, A.
Leuner, H.
Die toxische Ekstase, "Beiträge zur Ekstase" Edited by Th. Spoerri, in Bibl. psychiat. neurol., No. 134, pp. 73–114. Basel and New York, 1968.
Lind, Jens
Om Lægeplanter i danske Lægebøger og Klosterhaver Copenhagen, 1918.

Lindemark, Otto
Vore giftige blomsterplanter, 2nd Edition Co-
penhagen, 1970.
Linderholm, Emanuel
De stora haexprocesserna i Sverige Uppsala,
1918.
Marzell, Heinrich
*Zauberpflanzen, Hexentränke—Brauchtum
und Aberglaube* Stuttgart, 1964.
Mathison, Richard R.
The Eternal Search New York, 1958.
Murray, Margaret Alice
The Witch-Cult in Western Europe Oxford,
1921.
The God of the Witches London, 1933.
Nielsen, Harald
Lægeplanter og trolddomsurter Copenhagen,
1965.
Ovid
Metamorphoses Translated by F. J. Miller.
Loeb Classical Library, I–II, London, 1916.
Paulli, Simon
Flora Danica, Det er: Dansk Urtebog Copen-
hagen, 1648. Photographic reprint in 3 vols. with
introduction and commentaries by Johan Lange
and Vilh. Møller-Christensen. Copenhagen,
1971–72.
Perger, A. R. v.
Deutsche Pflanzensagen Stuttgart, 1864.
Peuckert, Will-Erich
*Hexensalben, "Medizinischer Monatsspiegel,"
8th part* August 1960, pp. 169–174. Darmstadt,
1960.

"*Ergänzende Kapitel über das deutsche Hexenwesen*" in Baroja's *Die Hexen und ihre Welt* 1967, pp. 285–320.
Plinius (Secundus Caius)
   Natural History Translated by H. Rackham, W..H. S. Jones and D. E. Eichholz. Loeb Classical Library, I–X, London, 1938–62.
Robbins, Rossell Hope
   The Encyclopedia of Witchcraft and Demonology London, 1959.
Rostrup, E.
   Den Danske Flora. En populær Vejledning..., *17th Ed.* Edited by C. A. Jørgensen. Copenhagen, 1947.
Smid, Henrick
   En skøn lystig ny Urtegaardt..., 1577. Reprinted in Henrik Smith's Lægebog, I–VII, published with a terminal essay by Anna-Elizabeth Brade. Copenhagen, 1976.
   Enskøn lystig ny Urtegaard Republished by Skipper Chr. Madsen. Aalborg, 1923.
Soldan-Heppe
   Soldans Geschichte der Hexenprozesse, I–II Edited by Dr. Heinrich Heppe. Stuttgart, 1880.
Sprenger, James and Kramer, Heinrich
   see Kramer, Heinrich and Sprenger, James
Theophrastus
   Enquiry into Plants Translated by Sir Arthur Hort. Loeb Classical Library, I–II, London, 1916.
Wagner, Hildebert
   Rauschgift-Drogen 2nd Impression, Berlin, 1970.

Woodward, Marcus (pub.)
  Gerard's Herball. The Essense Thereof Distilled from the Edition of Th. Johnson, 1636
  London, 1927. 2nd Impression, 1971.
Xenophon
  Hellenica, Anabasis, Apology, and Symposium
  Translated by C. L. Brownson and O. J. Todd.
  Loeb Classical Library, I–III, London, 1921–22.

LIST OF ILLUSTRATIONS

Cover illustration
Witches' Brew. From Ulrich Molitor: *De lamiis et phitonicis mulieribus*, 1489.
Page ii
The witches' evil deeds. From Reinhard Lutz: *Warhafftige Zeitung von den Gottlosen Hexen*, 1571.
Page 17
Witches' Sabbat. From Johannes Prætorius: *Blockes-Berges Verrichtung*, 1668.
Page 24
Common Moonwort. From John Gerard: *The Herball or Generall Historie of Plantes*, Enlarged by Thomas Johnson, 1636.
Page 28
Mandrake. From Jacob Theodor Tabernaemontanus: *Neuw vollkemmentlich Kreüterbuch*, 1613.
Page 37
Female and male mandrake. From *The Greete Herball*, 1526.

INDEX